MW01064797

NICOTEXT

99 Classic TV-Series for People in a Hurry

All rights reserved
Without limiting the rights under copyright reserved above, no part of this publication may be repro-
duced, stored in or introduced into a retrieval system, or transmitted, in any form or by any means
(electronic, mechanical, photocopying, recording or otheriwise), without the prior written permission
of both the copyright owner and the below publisher of this book, except for the quotation of brief
passages in reviews. Any person who does any unauthorized act in relation to this publication may
be liable to criminal prosecution and civil claims for damages.

This book is sold subject to the condition that it shall not, by way of trade or otherwise, be lent, re-
sold, hired out, or otherwise circulated without the publisher's prior consent in any form of binding or
cover other than that in which it is publised and without a similar condition including this condition
being imposed on the subsequent purchaser.

The publisher and authors disclaim any liability that may result from the use of the information
contained in this book.

Text: Thomas Wengelewski

Copyright © NICOTEXT 2010 All rights reserved.
NICOTEXT part of Cladd media ltd.
www.nicotext.com
info@nicotext.com

Printed in Poland
ISBN: 978-91-86283-03-2

INDEX

Guess what? You now have the fantastic opportunity to make your own index. Use a pen while reading the book and write the page number next to the title. Genious, we know, but no need to thank us.

INDEX

INDEX

Sanford and Son

Fred Sanford is a junk dealer in Los Angeles. His wife Elizabeth died and he is left with his son Lamont. This could have been called "Let's Make Money on Black Stereotypes."

Fred is always trying to get rich and is haunted by his sister-in-law Esther.

"It's Godzilla!"

The ratings eventually fail along with Redd Foxx's heart every episode. Junk dealers everywhere mourn their 15-minutes of fame.

"You hear that, Elizabeth? I'm coming to join ya, honey!"

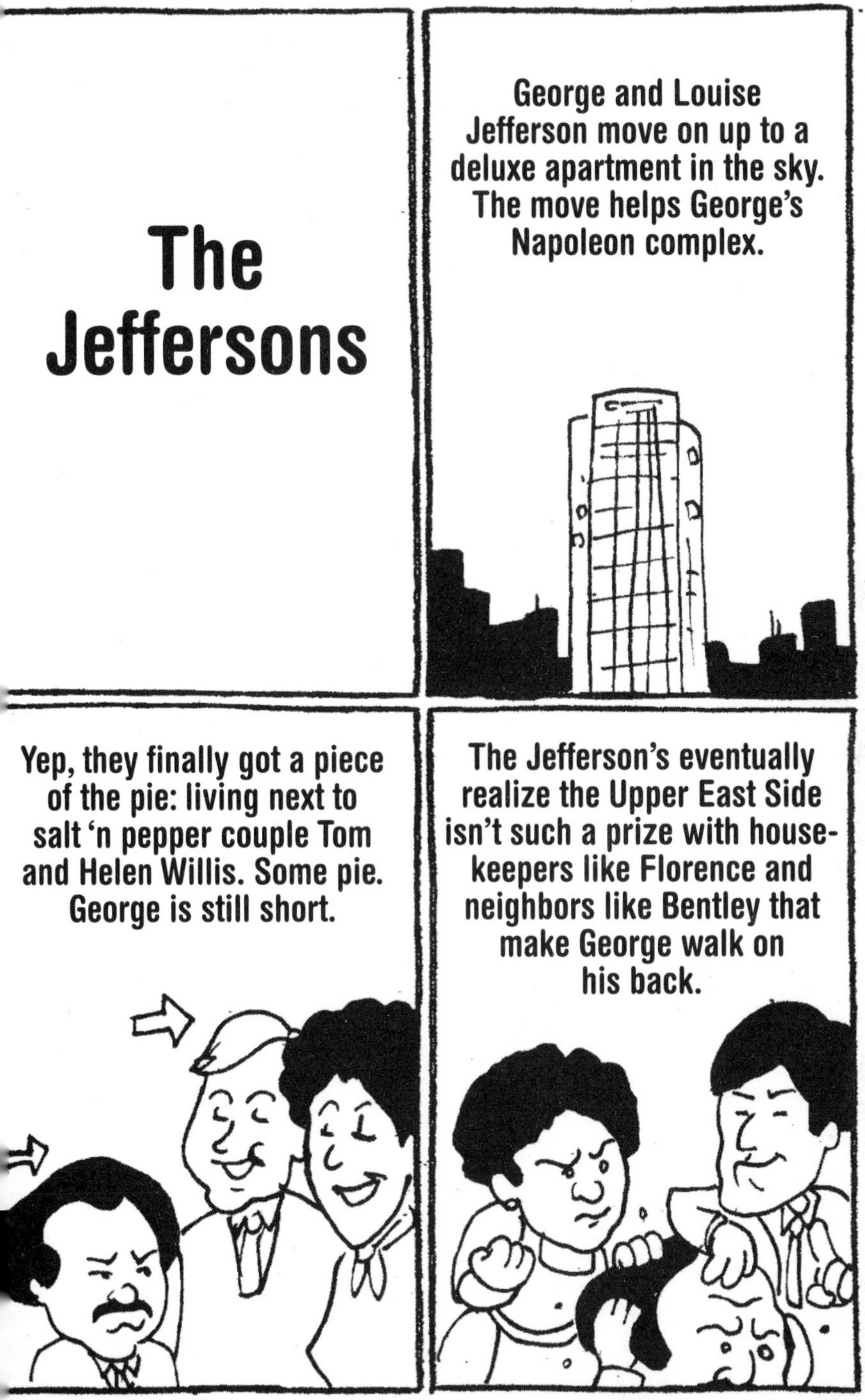

The Jeffersons
George and Louise Jefferson move on up to a deluxe apartment in the sky. The move helps George's Napoleon complex.
Yep, they finally got a piece of the pie: living next to salt 'n pepper couple Tom and Helen Willis. Some pie. George is still short.
The Jefferson's eventually realize the Upper East Side isn't such a prize with house-keepers like Florence and neighbors like Bentley that make George walk on his back.

Battlestar Galactica

Way out in a distant part of the universe called the Colonies humans are attacked by Cyclons and flee on the Battlestar Galactica.

But they can't flee the ho-hum ratings and the series is cancelled.

Or is it? Galactica comes back as the running humans come to Earth.

Basically to save money for sci-fi sets. This fails too. Score one for the Cyclons.

But those pesky humans are back in a new series battling the same Cyclons in space. But now they have a woman leader, a cool general, and some eye candy along with critical success. Finally Battlestar wins.

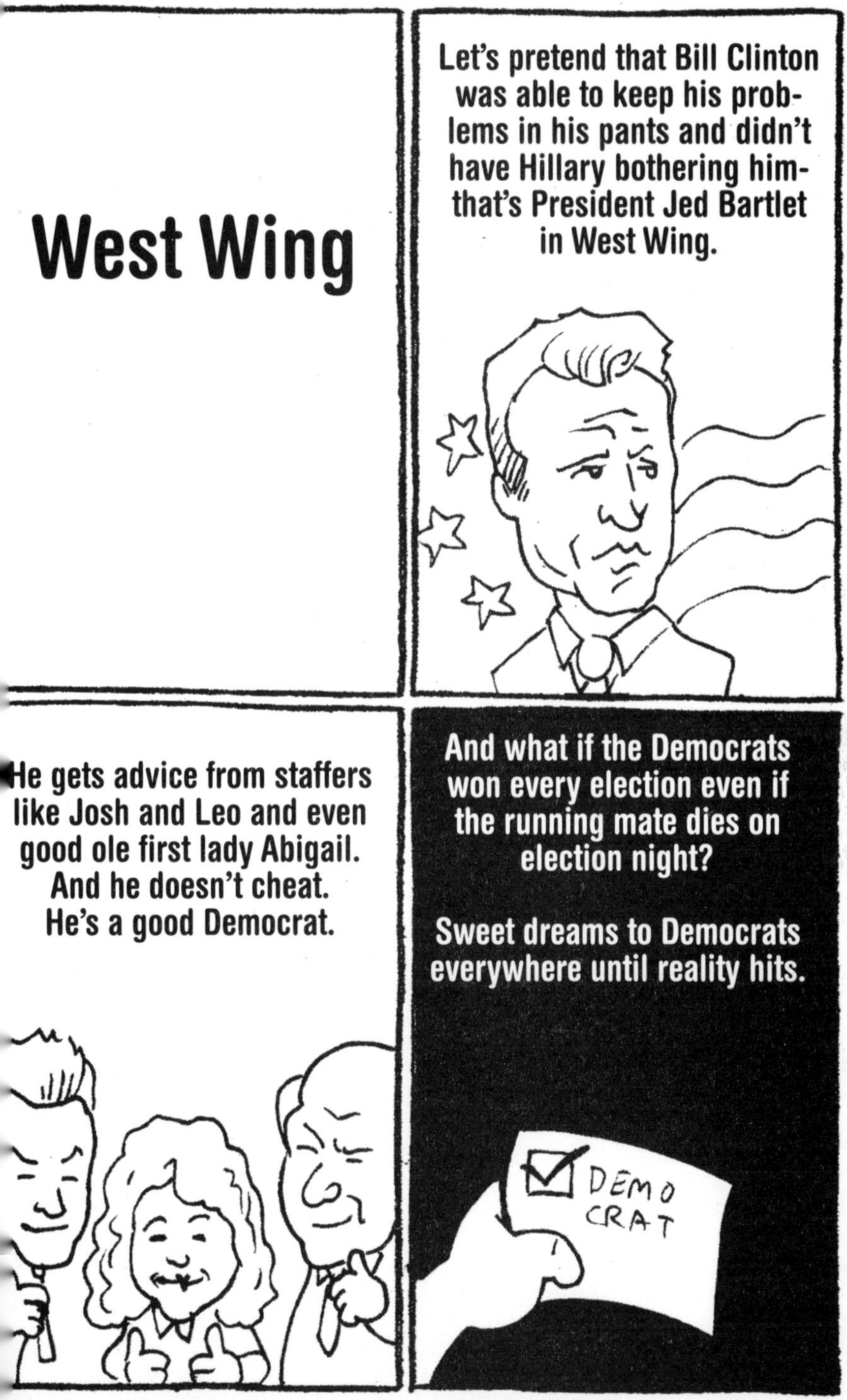
West Wing
Let's pretend that Bill Clinton was able to keep his problems in his pants and didn't have Hillary bothering him- that's President Jed Bartlet in West Wing.
He gets advice from staffers like Josh and Leo and even good ole first lady Abigail. And he doesn't cheat. He's a good Democrat.
And what if the Democrats won every election even if the running mate dies on election night?
Sweet dreams to Democrats everywhere until reality hits.
DEMOCRAT

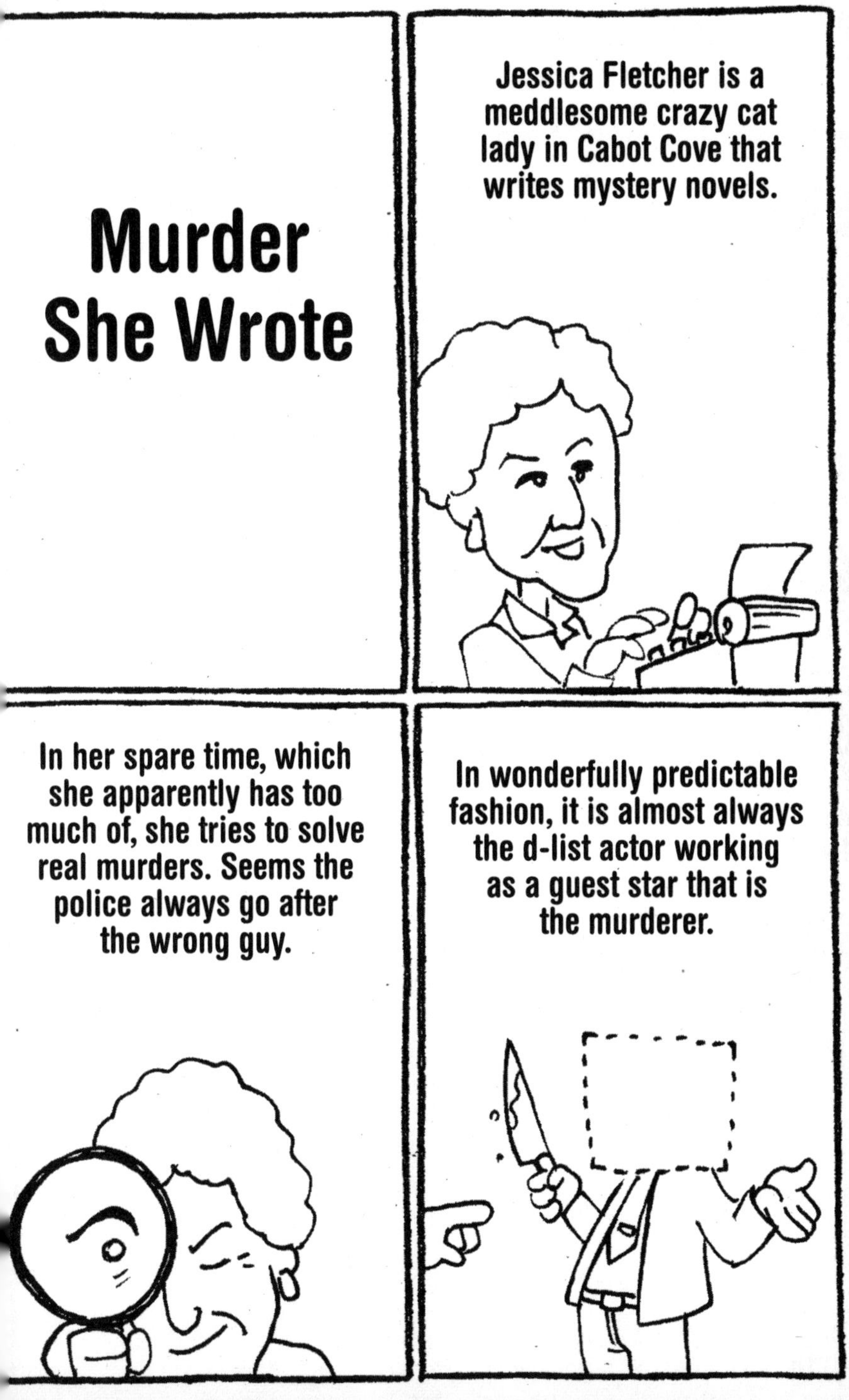
Murder She Wrote
Jessica Fletcher is a meddlesome crazy cat lady in Cabot Cove that writes mystery novels.
In her spare time, which she apparently has too much of, she tries to solve real murders. Seems the police always go after the wrong guy.
In wonderfully predictable fashion, it is almost always the d-list actor working as a guest star that is the murderer.

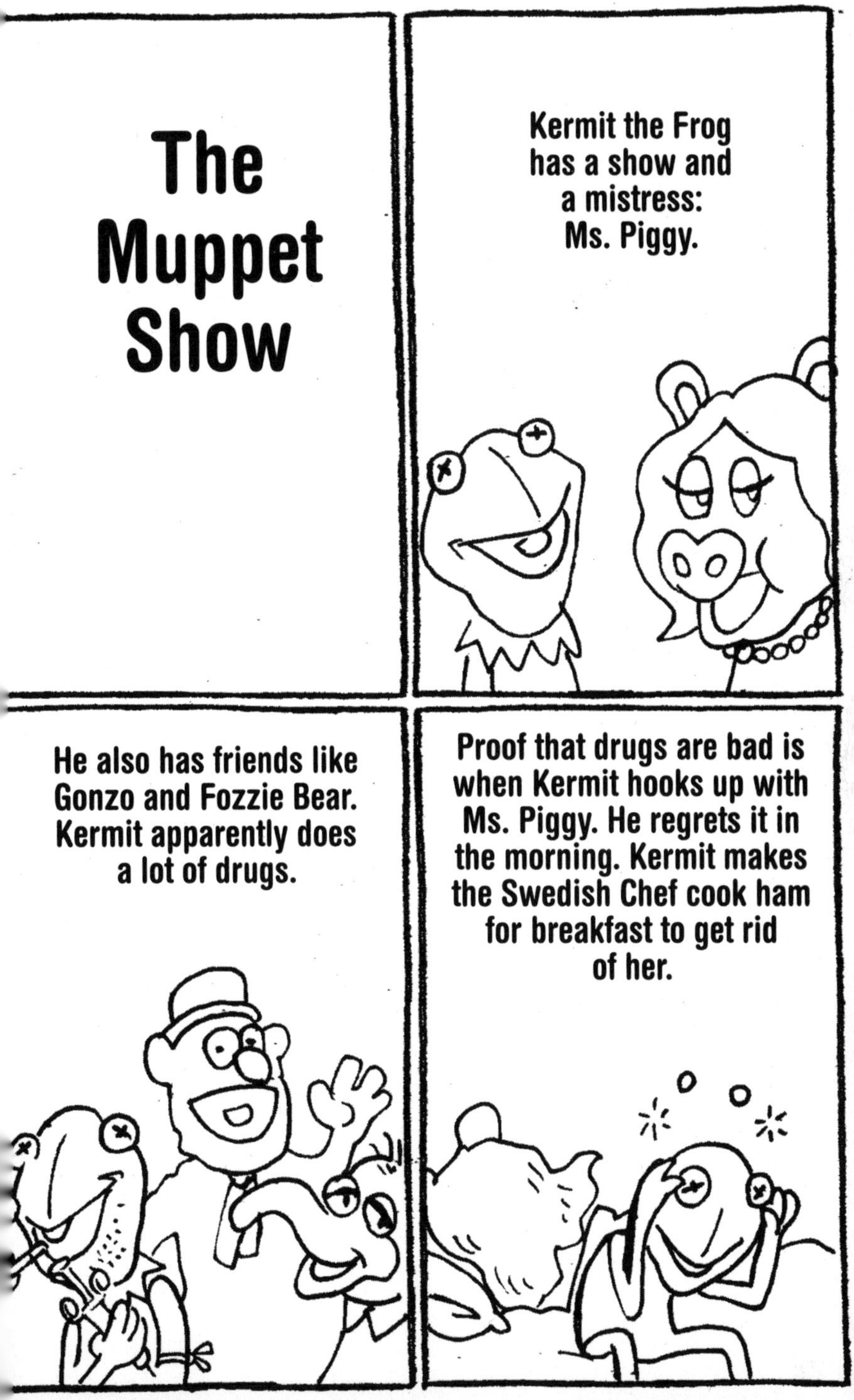
The Muppet Show
Kermit the Frog has a show and a mistress: Ms. Piggy.
He also has friends like Gonzo and Fozzie Bear. Kermit apparently does a lot of drugs.
Proof that drugs are bad is when Kermit hooks up with Ms. Piggy. He regrets it in the morning. Kermit makes the Swedish Chef cook ham for breakfast to get rid of her.

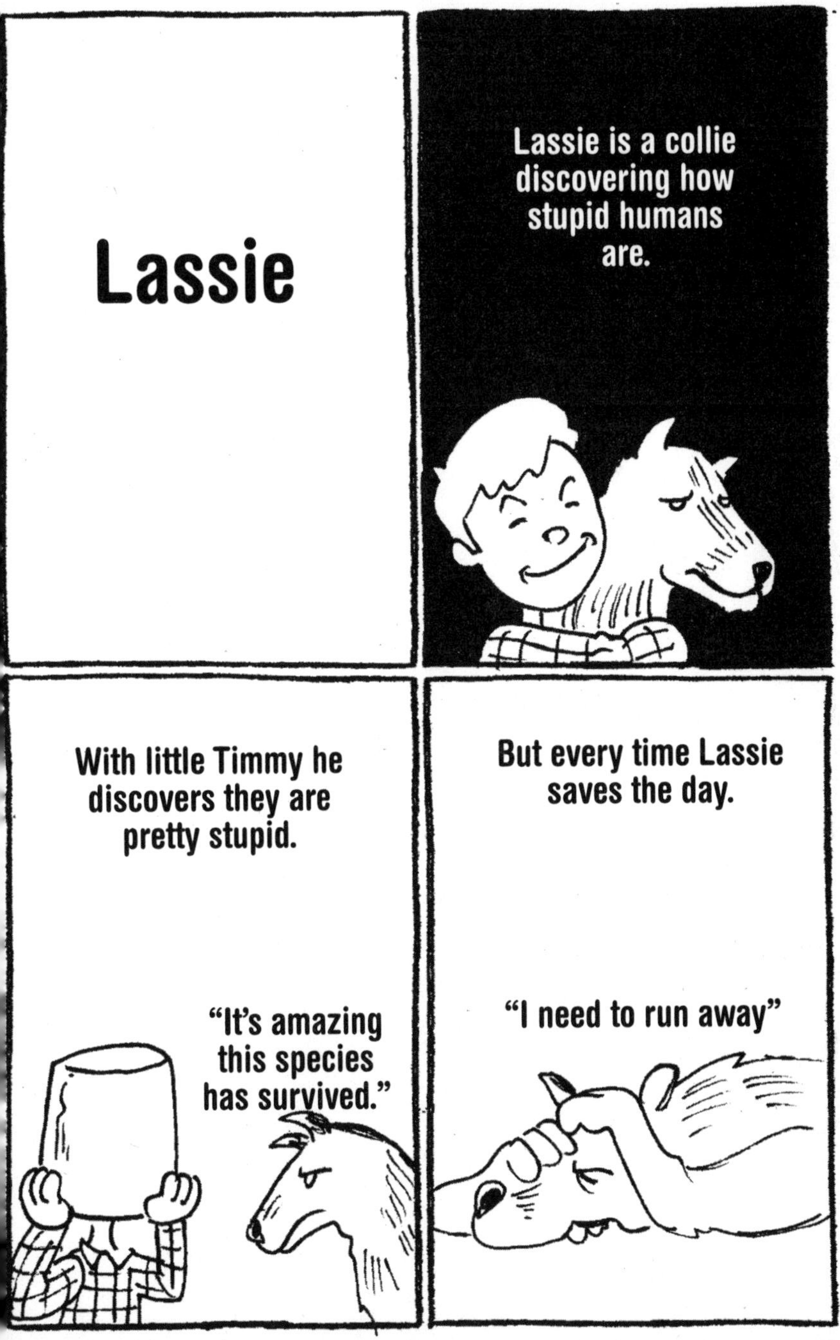
Lassie
Lassie is a collie discovering how stupid humans are.
With little Timmy he discovers they are pretty stupid.
"It's amazing this species has survived."
But every time Lassie saves the day.
"I need to run away"

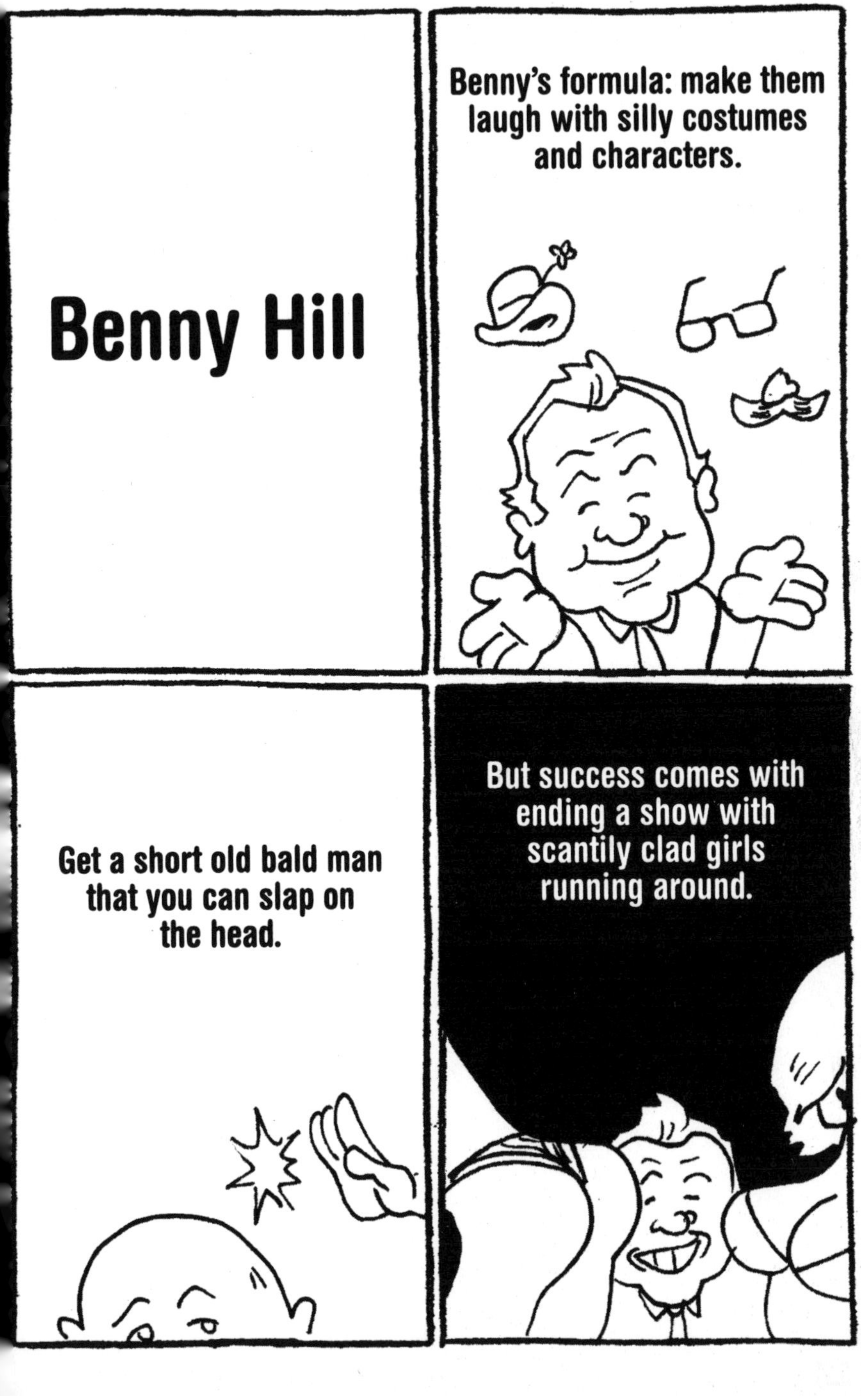
Benny Hill
Benny's formula: make them laugh with silly costumes and characters.
Get a short old bald man that you can slap on the head.
But success comes with ending a show with scantily clad girls running around.

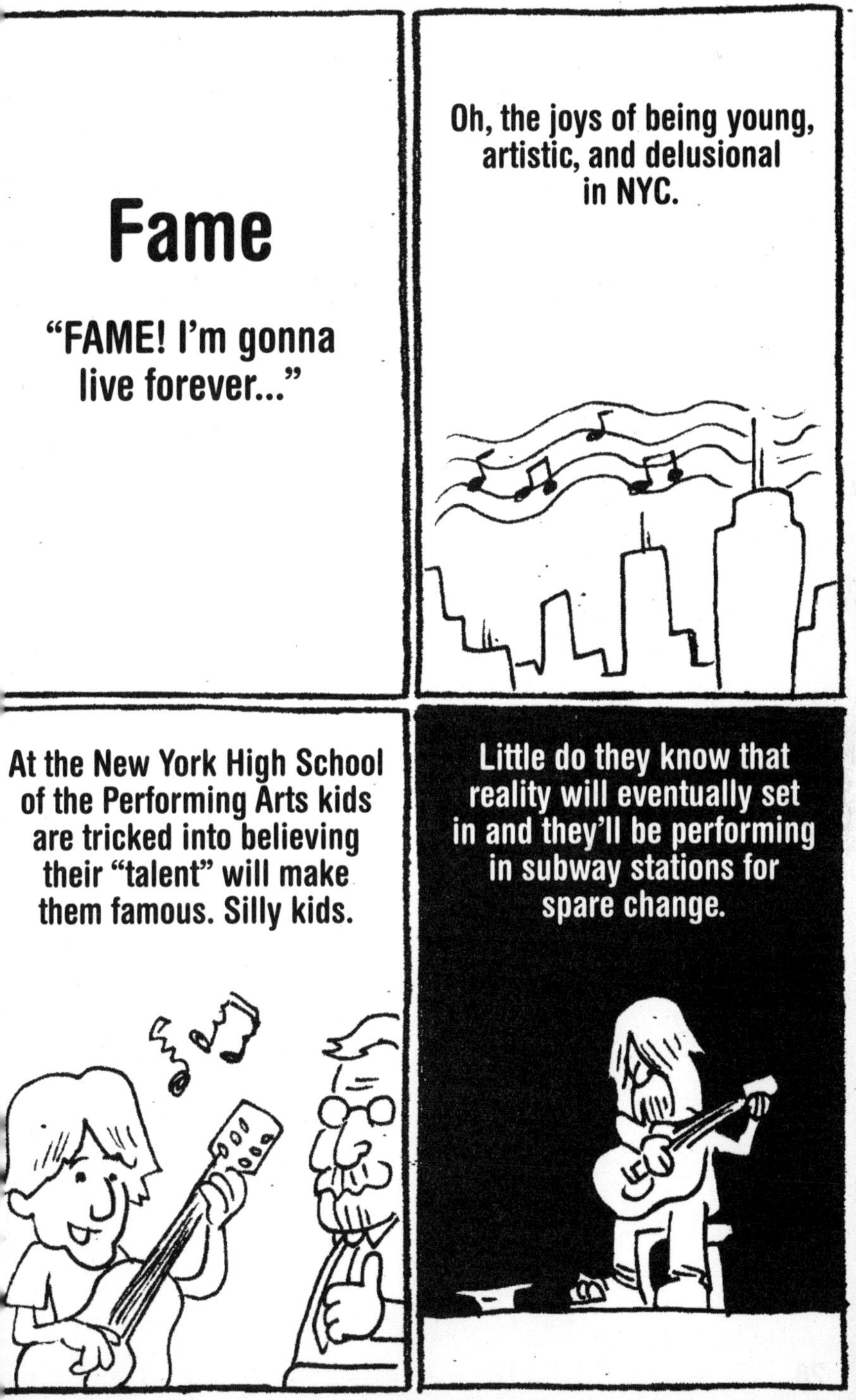
Fame
"FAME! I'm gonna live forever..."
Oh, the joys of being young, artistic, and delusional in NYC.
At the New York High School of the Performing Arts kids are tricked into believing their "talent" will make them famous. Silly kids.
Little do they know that reality will eventually set in and they'll be performing in subway stations for spare change.

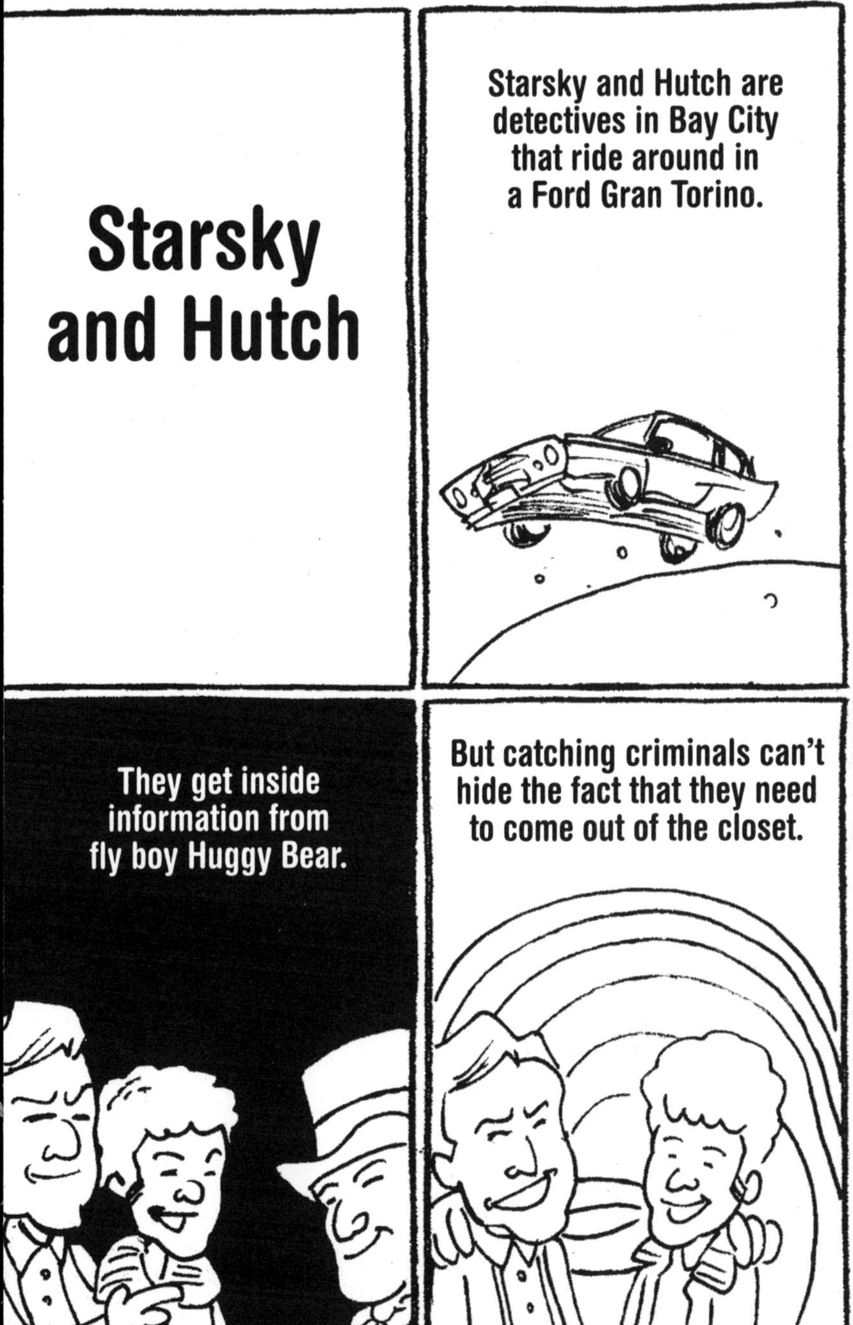
Starsky and Hutch
Starsky and Hutch are detectives in Bay City that ride around in a Ford Gran Torino.
They get inside information from fly boy Huggy Bear.
But catching criminals can't hide the fact that they need to come out of the closet.

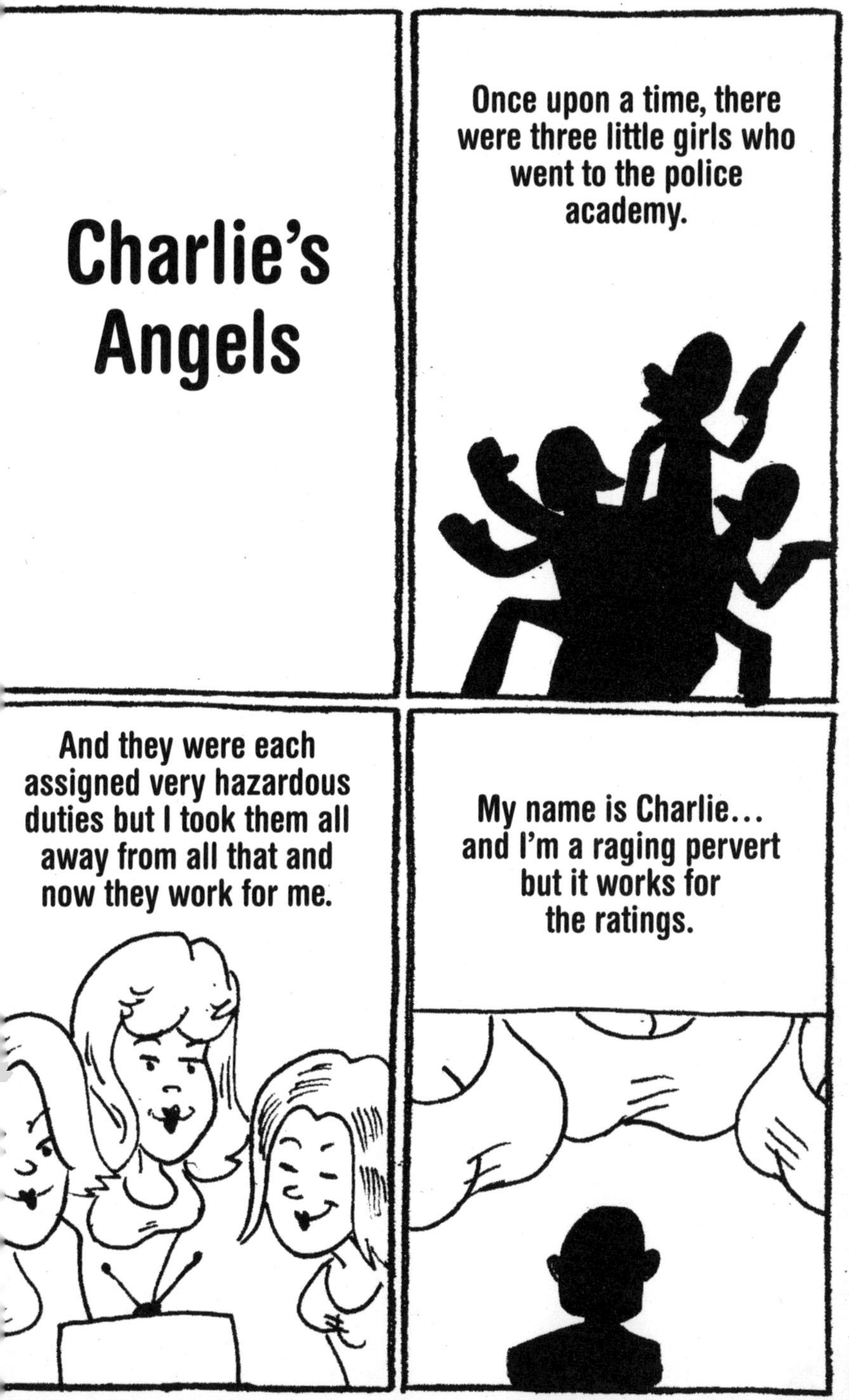
Charlie's Angels
Once upon a time, there were three little girls who went to the police academy.
And they were each assigned very hazardous duties but I took them all away from all that and now they work for me.
My name is Charlie… and I'm a raging pervert but it works for the ratings.

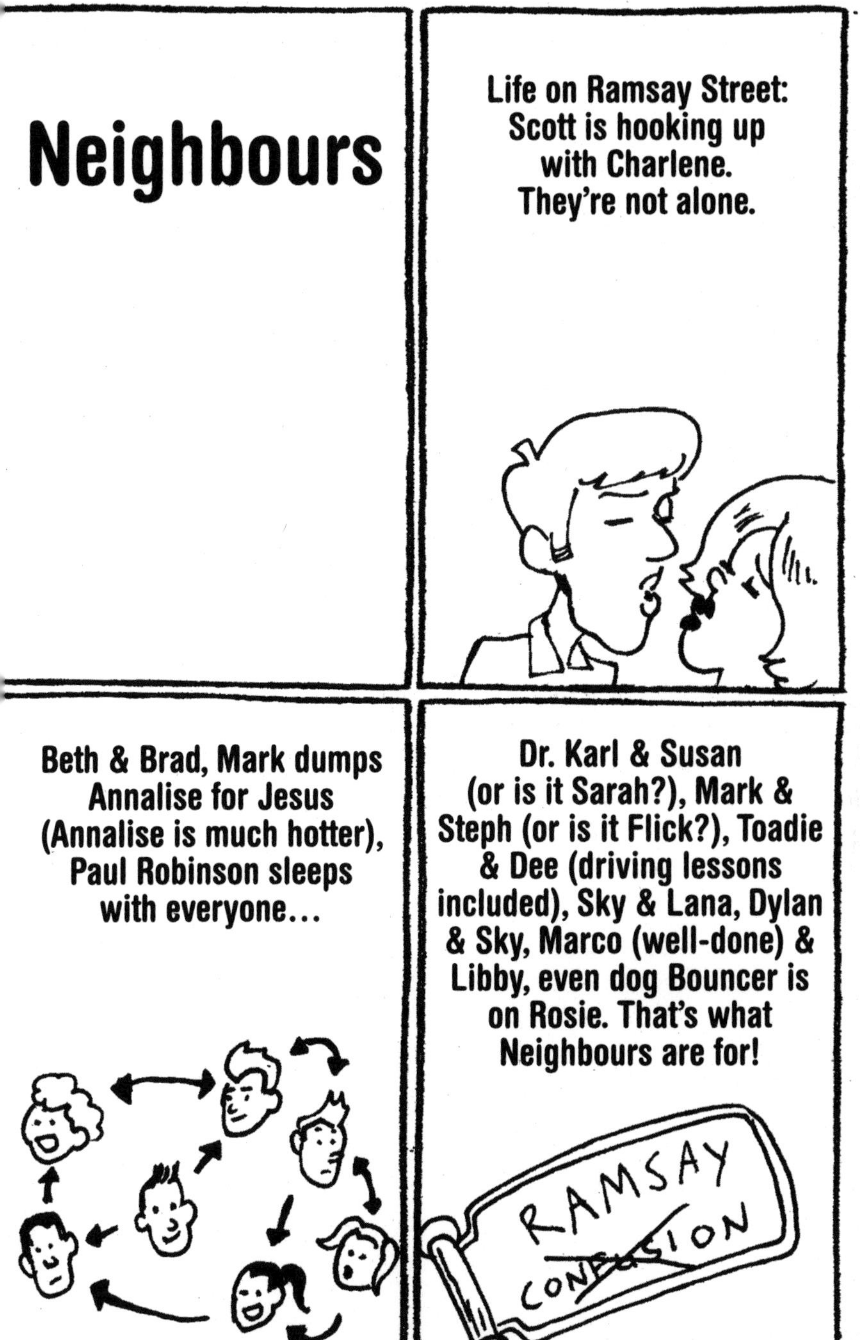

Neighbours
Life on Ramsay Street: Scott is hooking up with Charlene. They're not alone.
Beth & Brad, Mark dumps Annalise for Jesus (Annalise is much hotter), Paul Robinson sleeps with everyone…
Dr. Karl & Susan (or is it Sarah?), Mark & Steph (or is it Flick?), Toadie & Dee (driving lessons included), Sky & Lana, Dylan & Sky, Marco (well-done) & Libby, even dog Bouncer is on Rosie. That's what Neighbours are for!
RAMSAY
CONFUSION

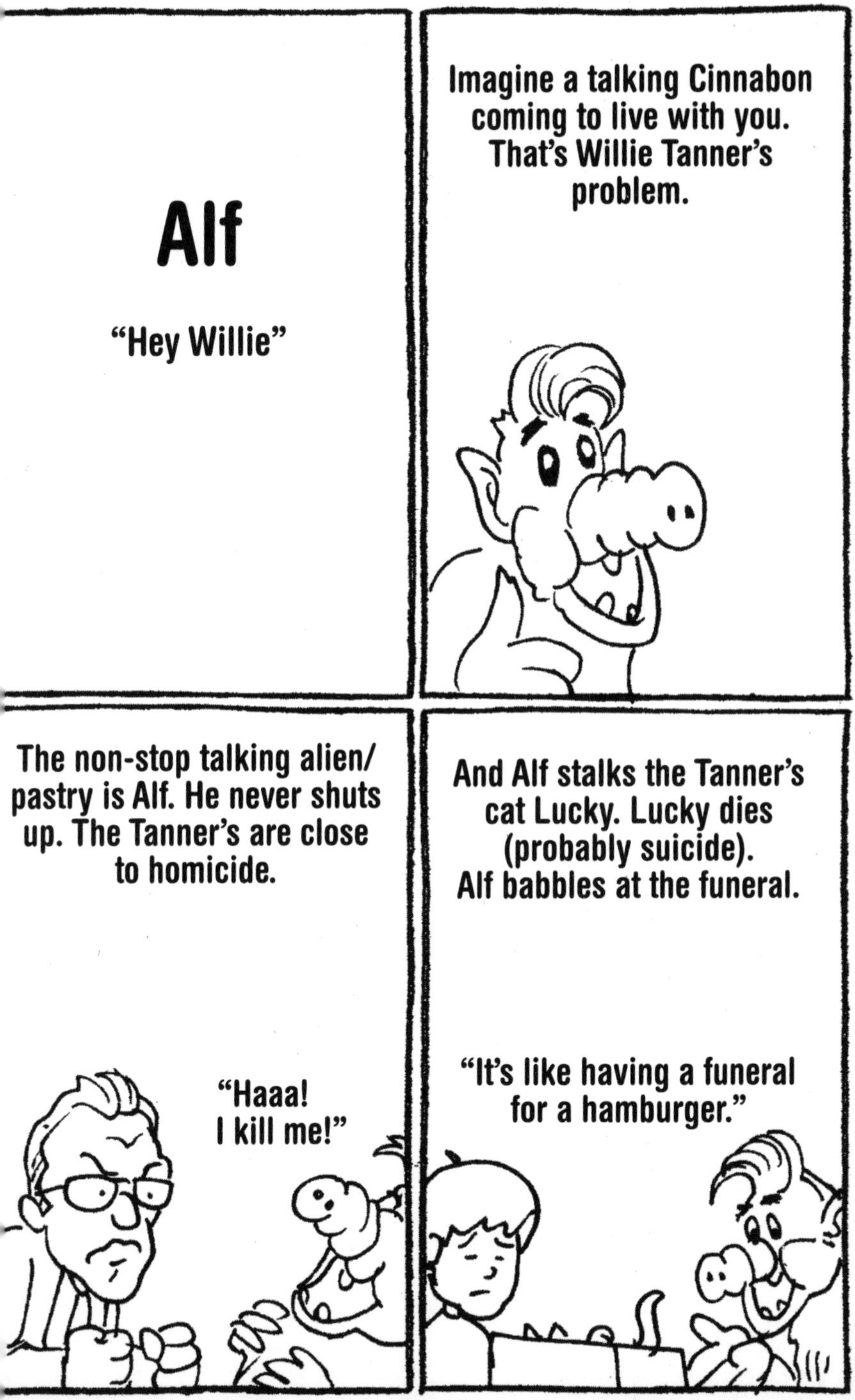
Alf
"Hey Willie"
Imagine a talking Cinnabon coming to live with you. That's Willie Tanner's problem.
The non-stop talking alien/ pastry is Alf. He never shuts up. The Tanner's are close to homicide.
"Haaa! I kill me!"
And Alf stalks the Tanner's cat Lucky. Lucky dies (probably suicide). Alf babbles at the funeral.
"It's like having a funeral for a hamburger."

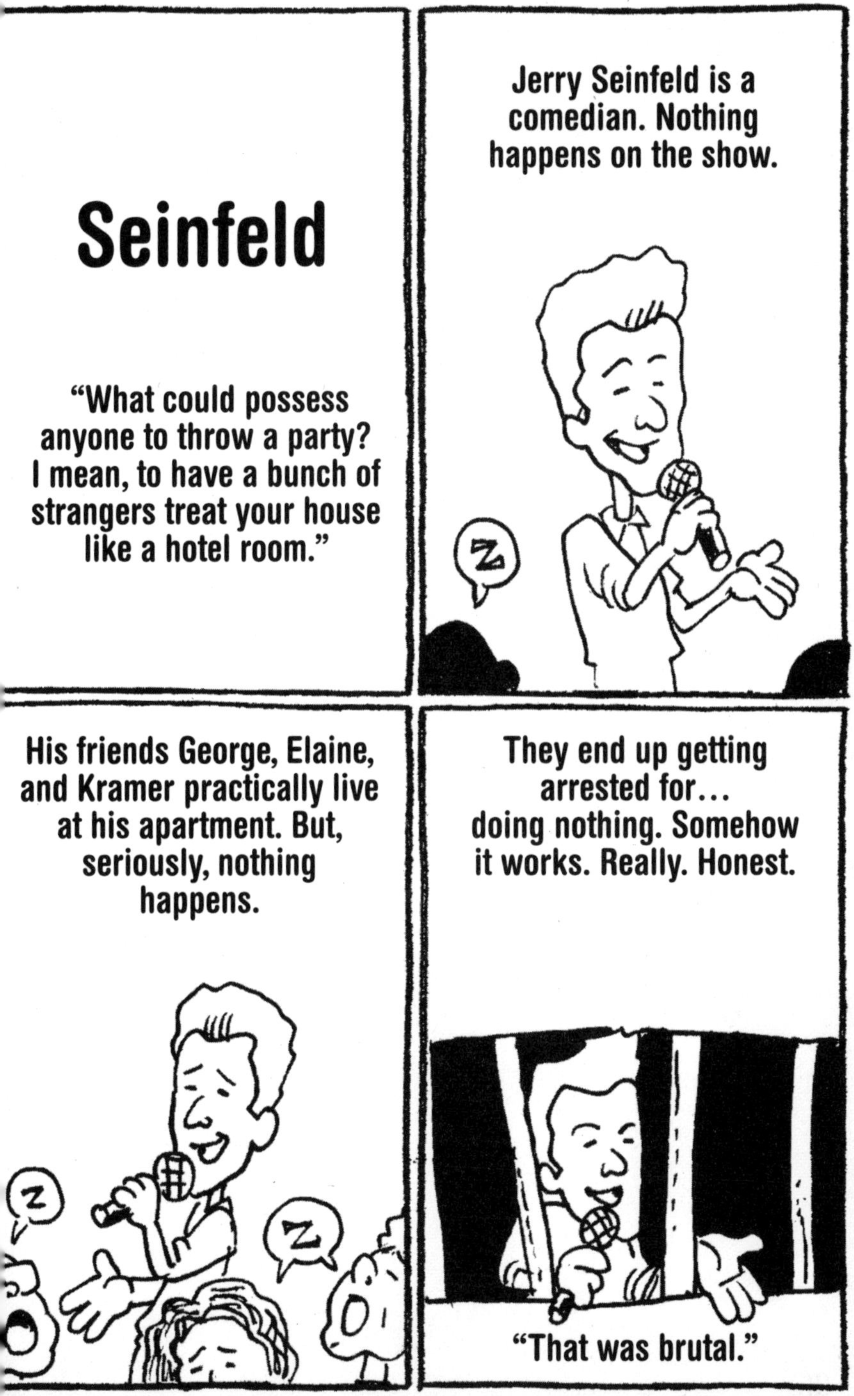

Seinfeld
"What could possess anyone to throw a party? I mean, to have a bunch of strangers treat your house like a hotel room."
Jerry Seinfeld is a comedian. Nothing happens on the show.
Z
His friends George, Elaine, and Kramer practically live at his apartment. But, seriously, nothing happens.
Z
Z
They end up getting arrested for... doing nothing. Somehow it works. Really. Honest.
"That was brutal."

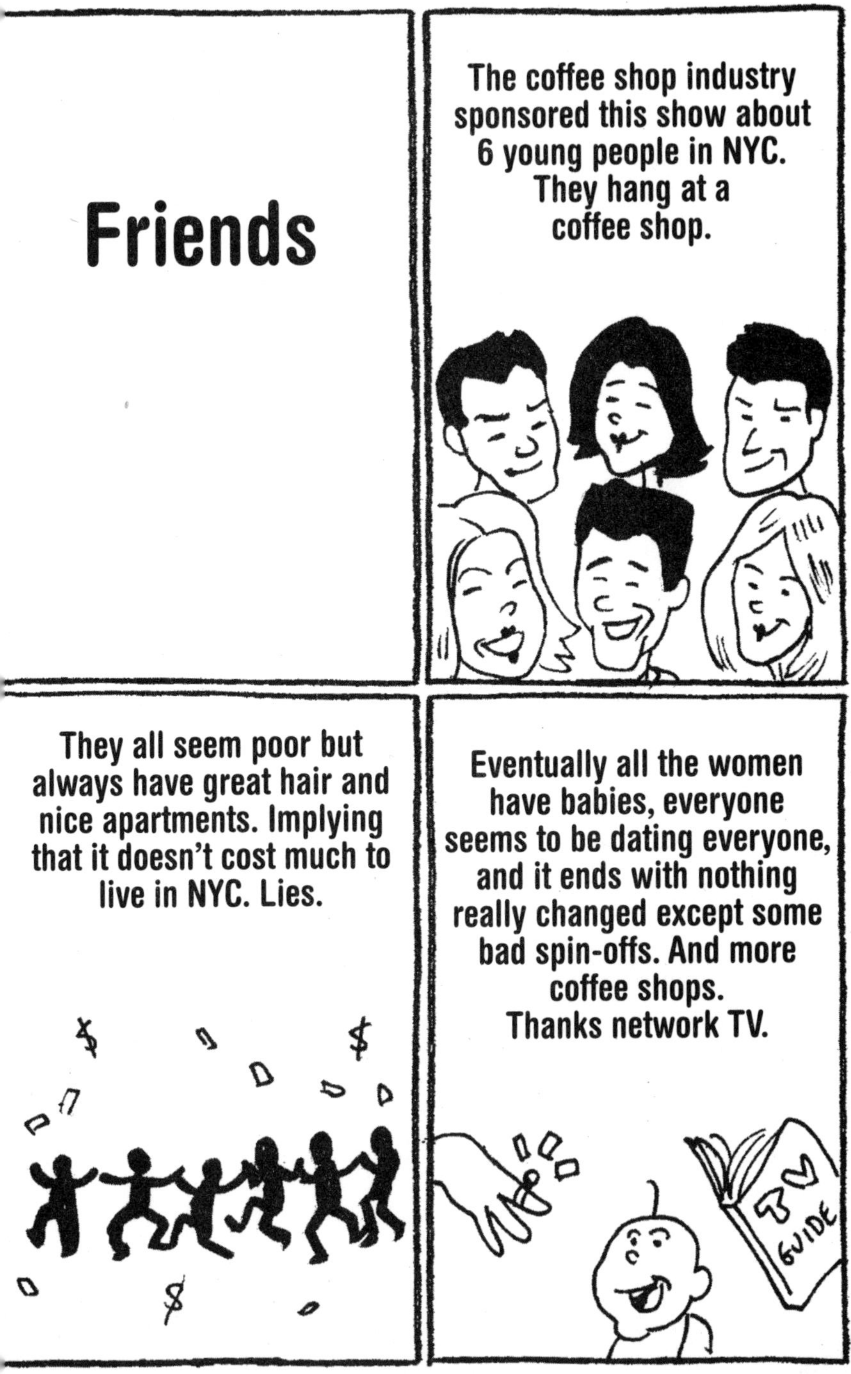
Friends
The coffee shop industry sponsored this show about 6 young people in NYC. They hang at a coffee shop.
They all seem poor but always have great hair and nice apartments. Implying that it doesn't cost much to live in NYC. Lies.
Eventually all the women have babies, everyone seems to be dating everyone, and it ends with nothing really changed except some bad spin-offs. And more coffee shops. Thanks network TV.
TV GUIDE

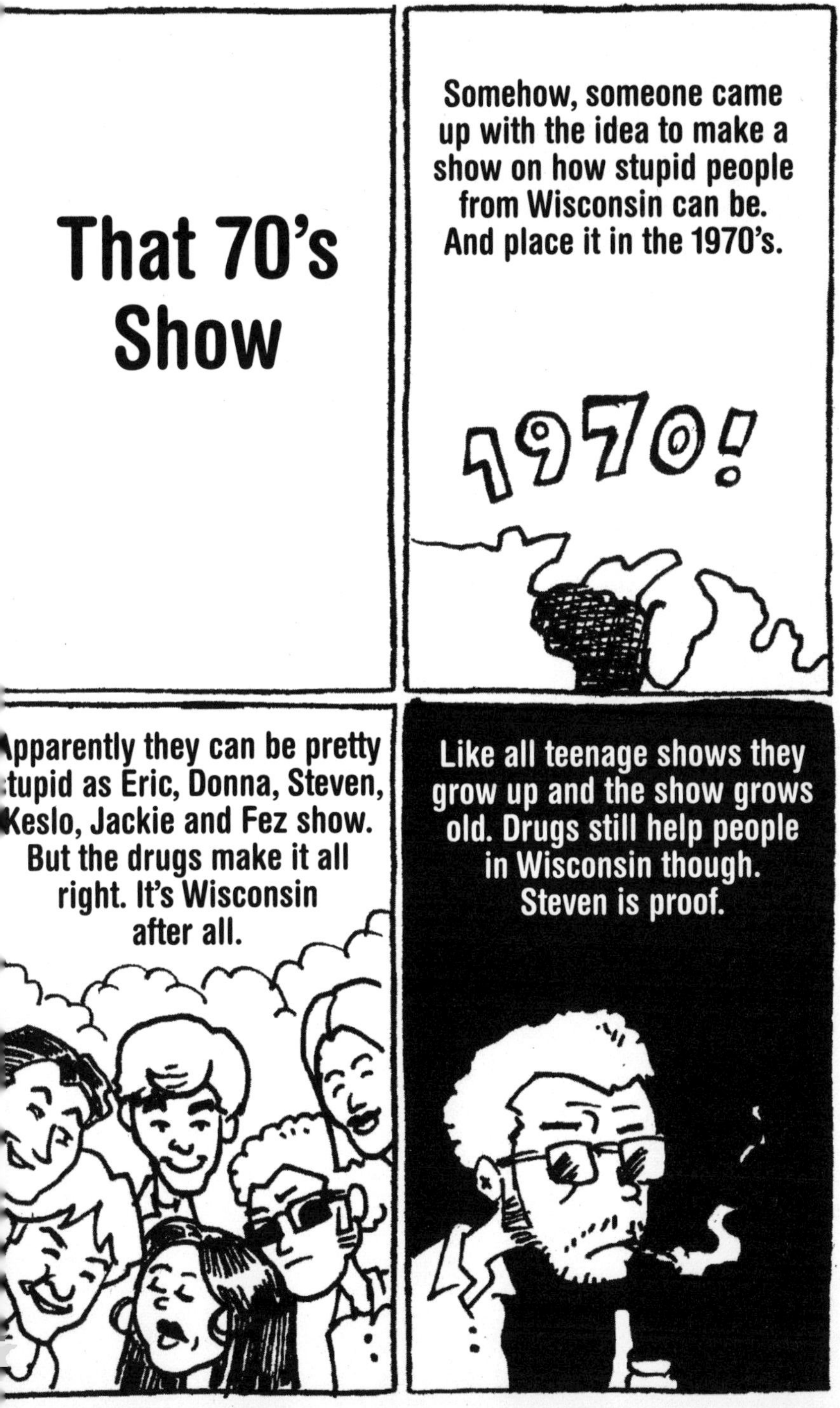
That 70's Show
Somehow, someone came up with the idea to make a show on how stupid people from Wisconsin can be. And place it in the 1970's.
1970!
pparently they can be pretty tupid as Eric, Donna, Steven, Keslo, Jackie and Fez show. But the drugs make it all right. It's Wisconsin after all.
Like all teenage shows they grow up and the show grows old. Drugs still help people in Wisconsin though. Steven is proof.

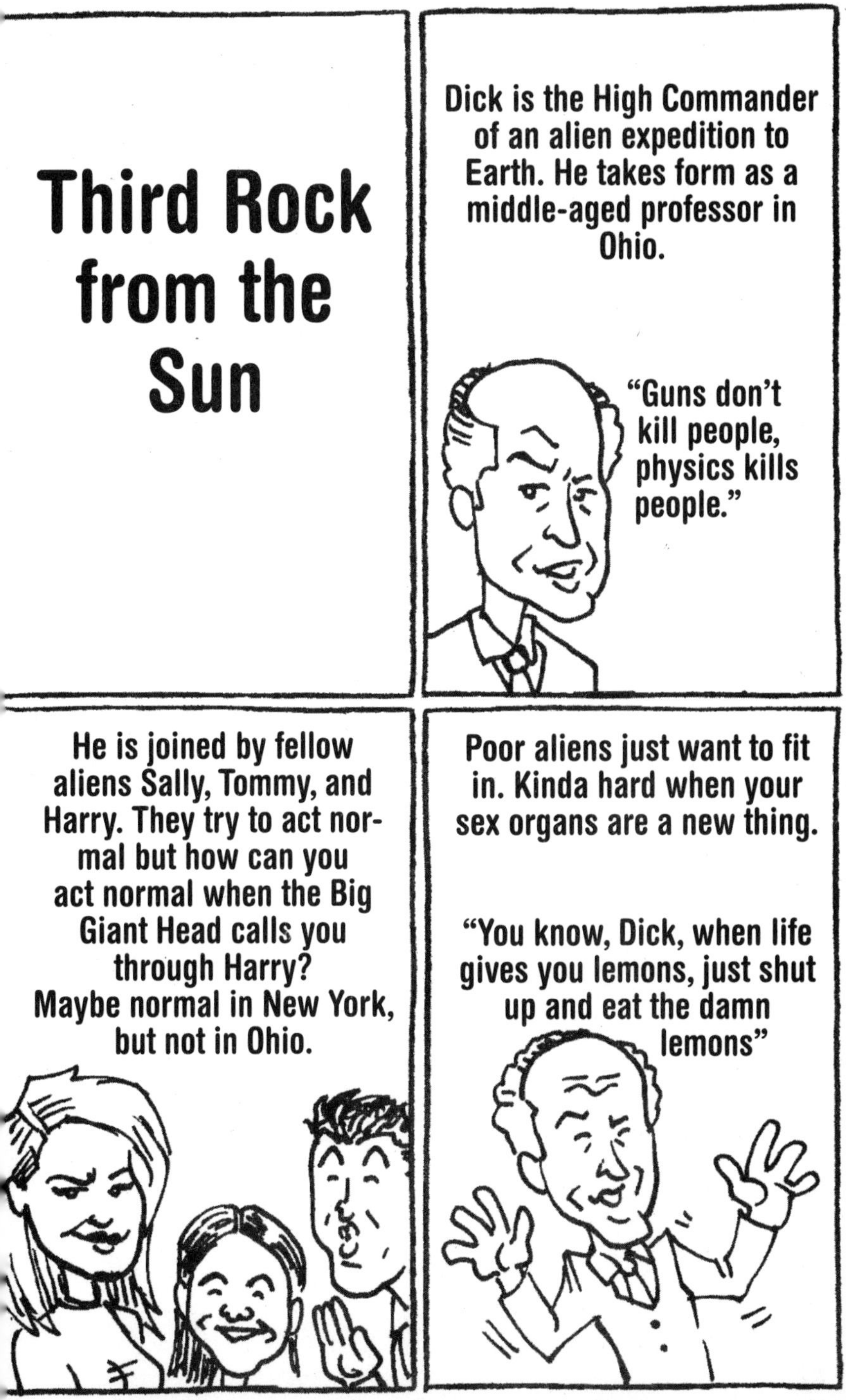
Third Rock from the Sun
Dick is the High Commander of an alien expedition to Earth. He takes form as a middle-aged professor in Ohio.
"Guns don't kill people, physics kills people."
He is joined by fellow aliens Sally, Tommy, and Harry. They try to act nor-mal but how can you act normal when the Big Giant Head calls you through Harry? Maybe normal in New York, but not in Ohio.
Poor aliens just want to fit in. Kinda hard when your sex organs are a new thing.
"You know, Dick, when life gives you lemons, just shut up and eat the damn lemons"

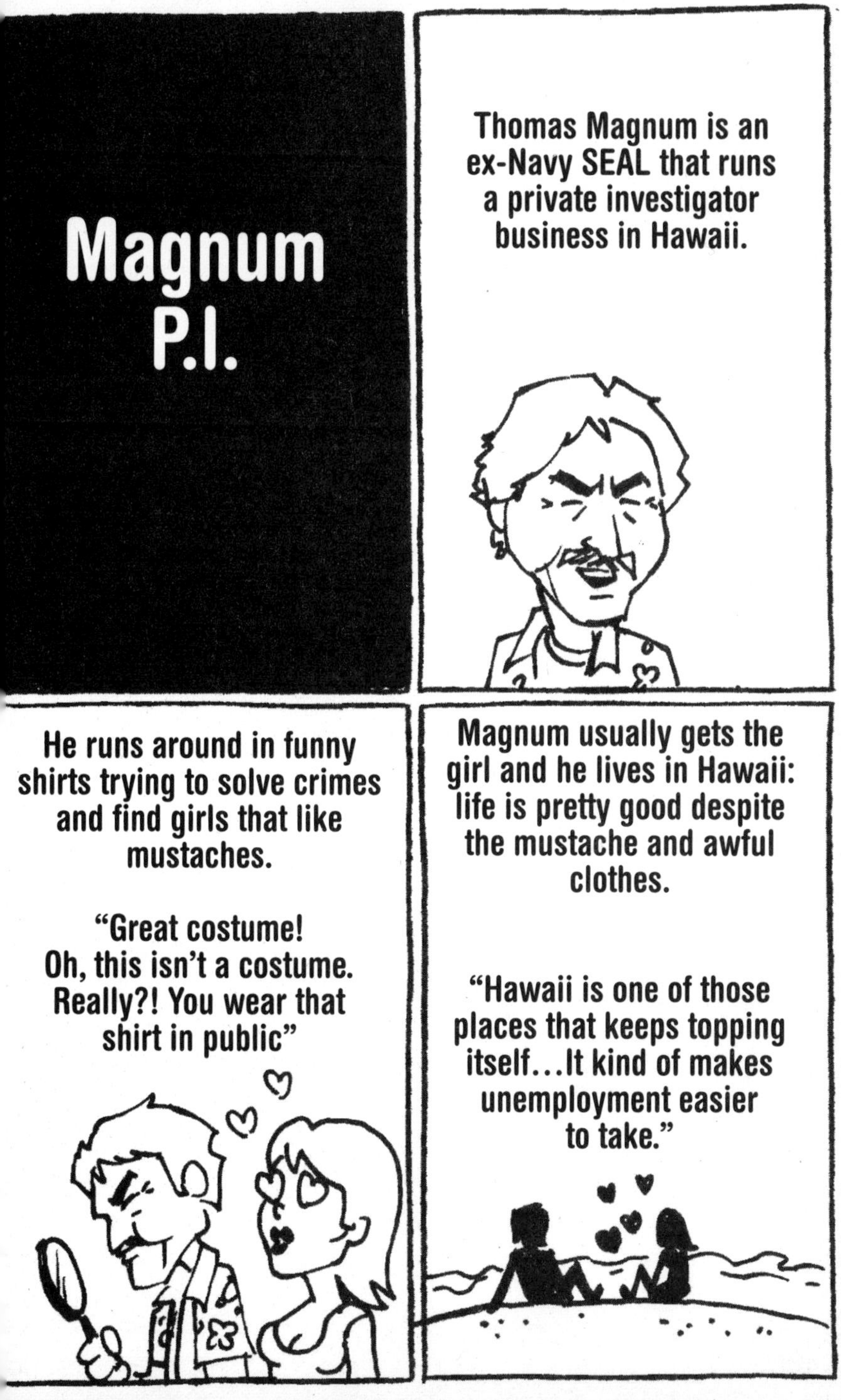
Magnum P.I.
Thomas Magnum is an ex-Navy SEAL that runs a private investigator business in Hawaii.
He runs around in funny shirts trying to solve crimes and find girls that like mustaches.
“Great costume! Oh, this isn’t a costume. Really?! You wear that shirt in public”
Magnum usually gets the girl and he lives in Hawaii: life is pretty good despite the mustache and awful clothes.
“Hawaii is one of those places that keeps topping itself…It kind of makes unemployment easier to take.”

44

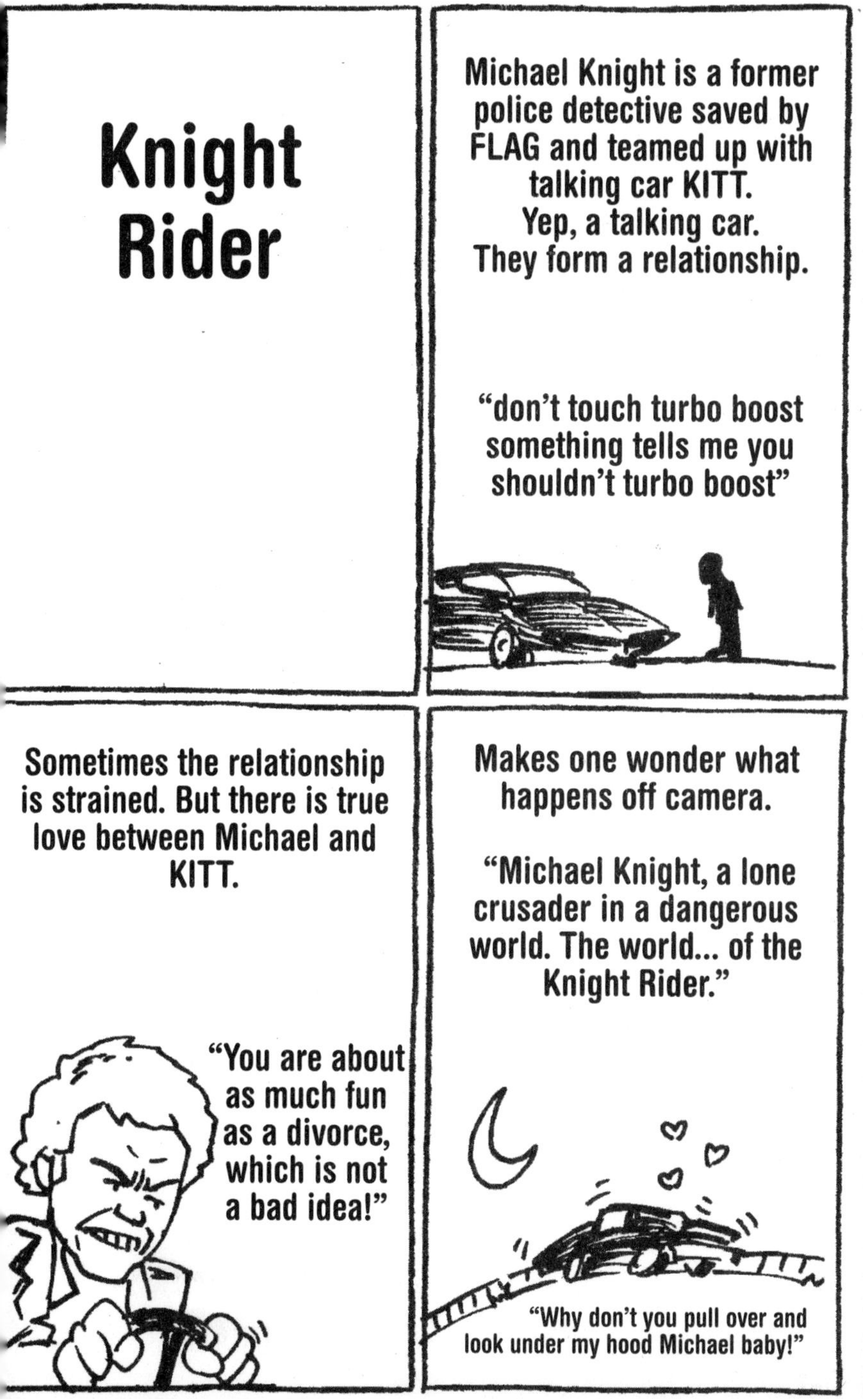

Knight Rider
Michael Knight is a former police detective saved by FLAG and teamed up with talking car KITT. Yep, a talking car. They form a relationship.
"don't touch turbo boost something tells me you shouldn't turbo boost"
Sometimes the relationship is strained. But there is true love between Michael and KITT.
"You are about as much fun as a divorce, which is not a bad idea!"
Makes one wonder what happens off camera.
"Michael Knight, a lone crusader in a dangerous world. The world... of the Knight Rider."
"Why don't you pull over and look under my hood Michael baby!"

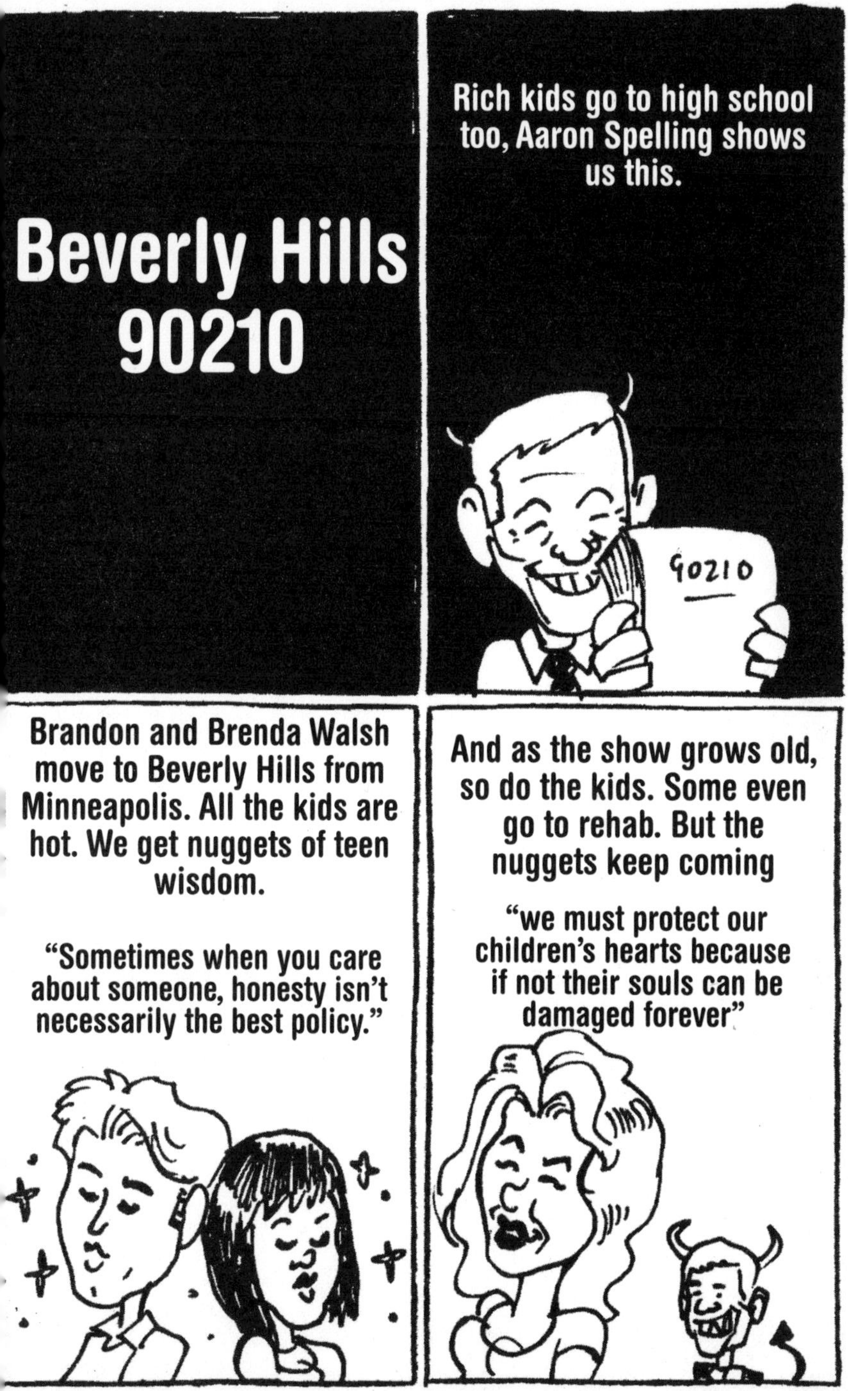
Beverly Hills 90210
Rich kids go to high school too, Aaron Spelling shows us this.
90210
Brandon and Brenda Walsh move to Beverly Hills from Minneapolis. All the kids are hot. We get nuggets of teen wisdom.
"Sometimes when you care about someone, honesty isn't necessarily the best policy."
And as the show grows old, so do the kids. Some even go to rehab. But the nuggets keep coming
"we must protect our children's hearts because if not their souls can be damaged forever"

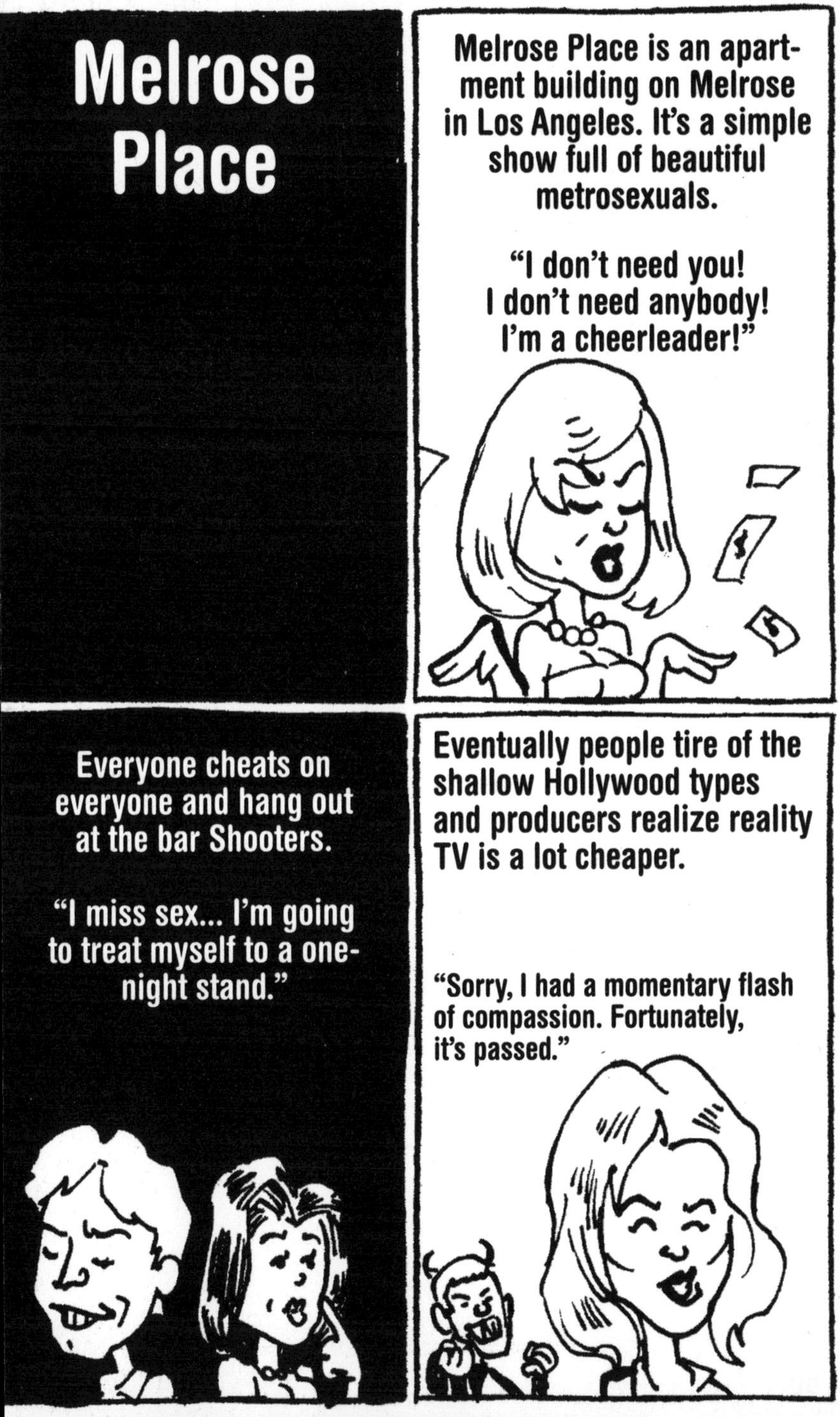
Melrose Place
Melrose Place is an apartment building on Melrose in Los Angeles. It's a simple show full of beautiful metrosexuals.
"I don't need you! I don't need anybody! I'm a cheerleader!"
Everyone cheats on everyone and hang out at the bar Shooters.
"I miss sex... I'm going to treat myself to a one-night stand."
Eventually people tire of the shallow Hollywood types and producers realize reality TV is a lot cheaper.
"Sorry, I had a momentary flash of compassion. Fortunately, it's passed."

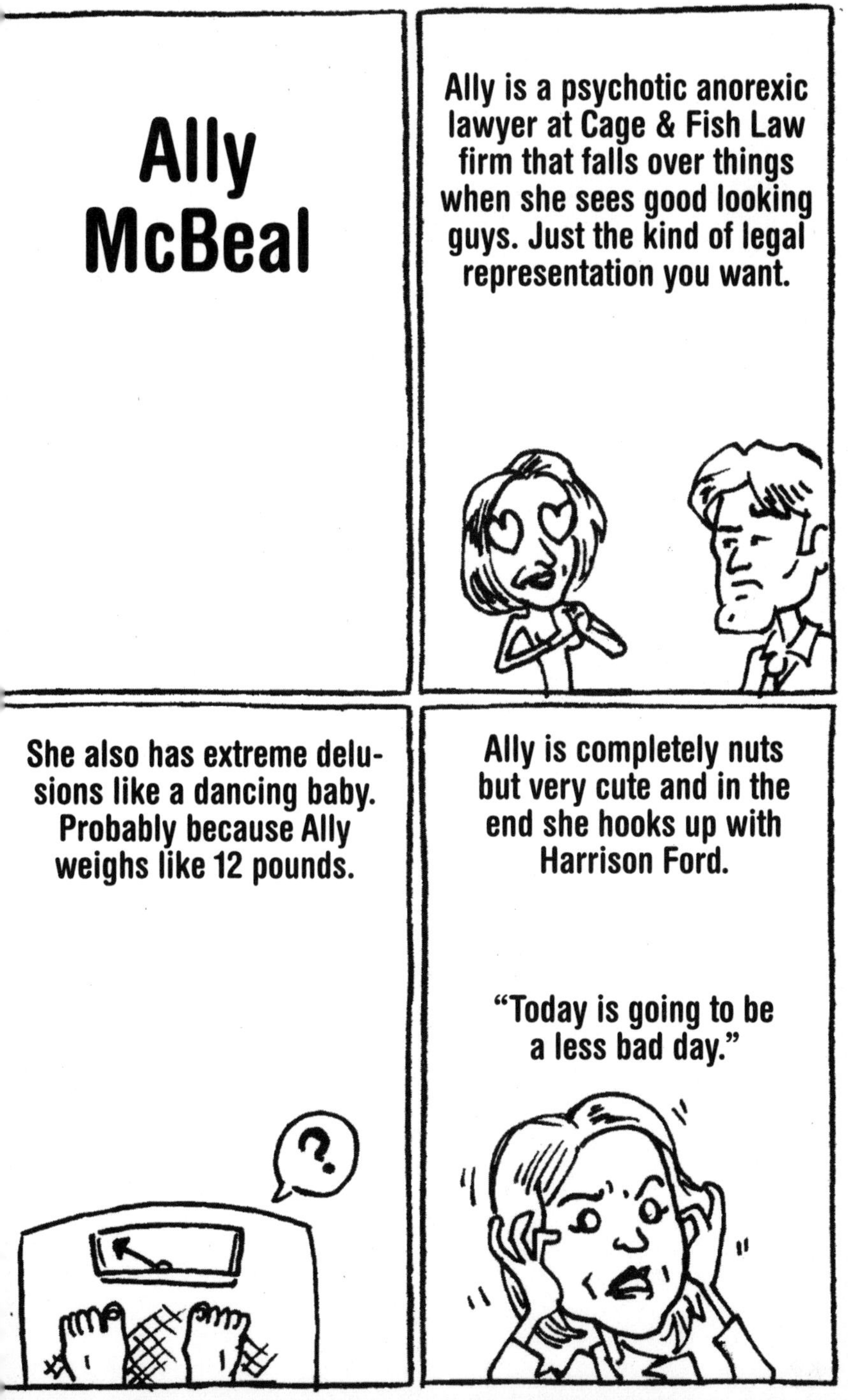
Ally McBeal
Ally is a psychotic anorexic lawyer at Cage & Fish Law firm that falls over things when she sees good looking guys. Just the kind of legal representation you want.
She also has extreme delusions like a dancing baby. Probably because Ally weighs like 12 pounds.
?
Ally is completely nuts but very cute and in the end she hooks up with Harrison Ford.
"Today is going to be a less bad day."

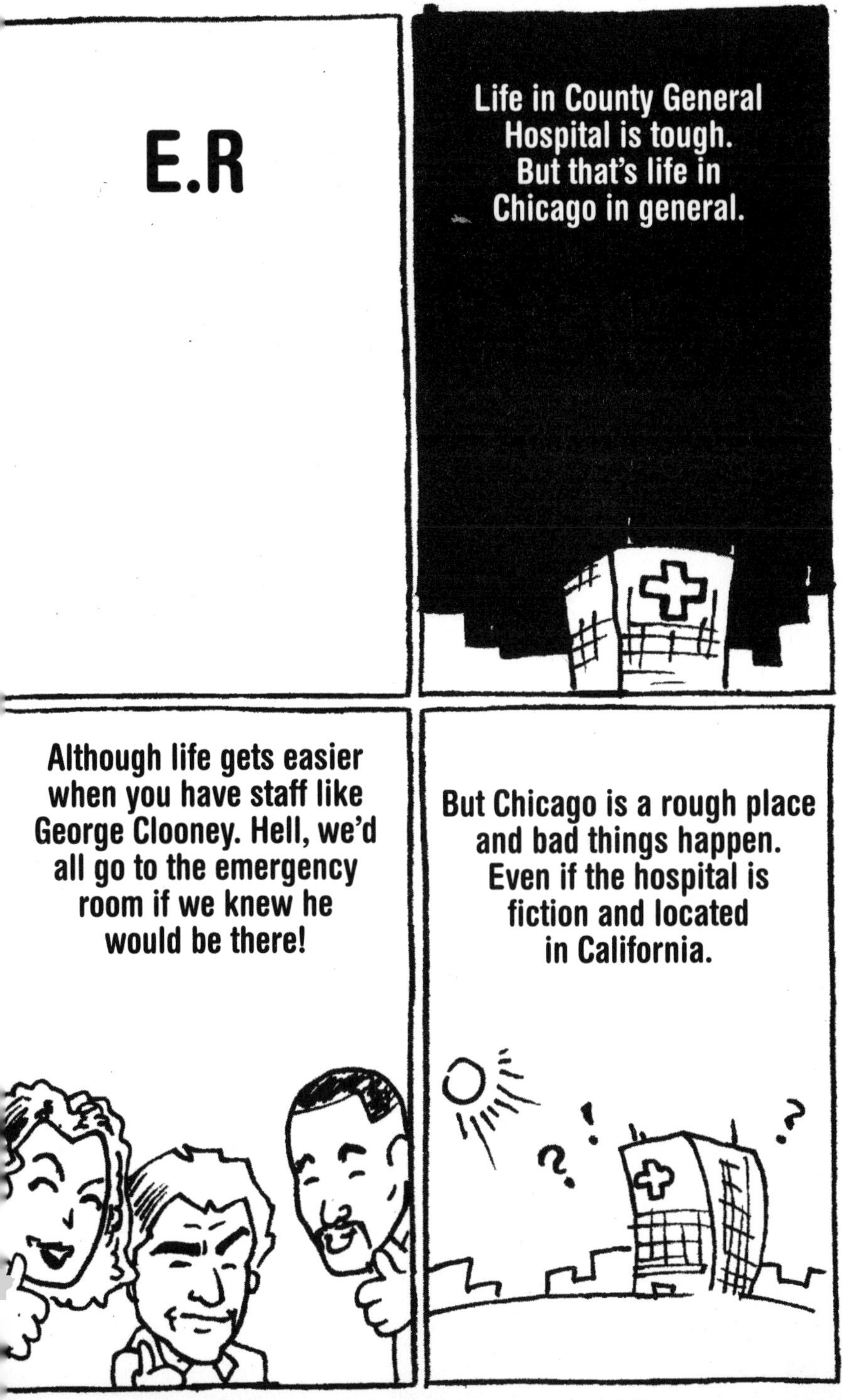
E.R
Life in County General Hospital is tough. But that's life in Chicago in general.
Although life gets easier when you have staff like George Clooney. Hell, we'd all go to the emergency room if we knew he would be there!
But Chicago is a rough place and bad things happen. Even if the hospital is fiction and located in California.
?!
?

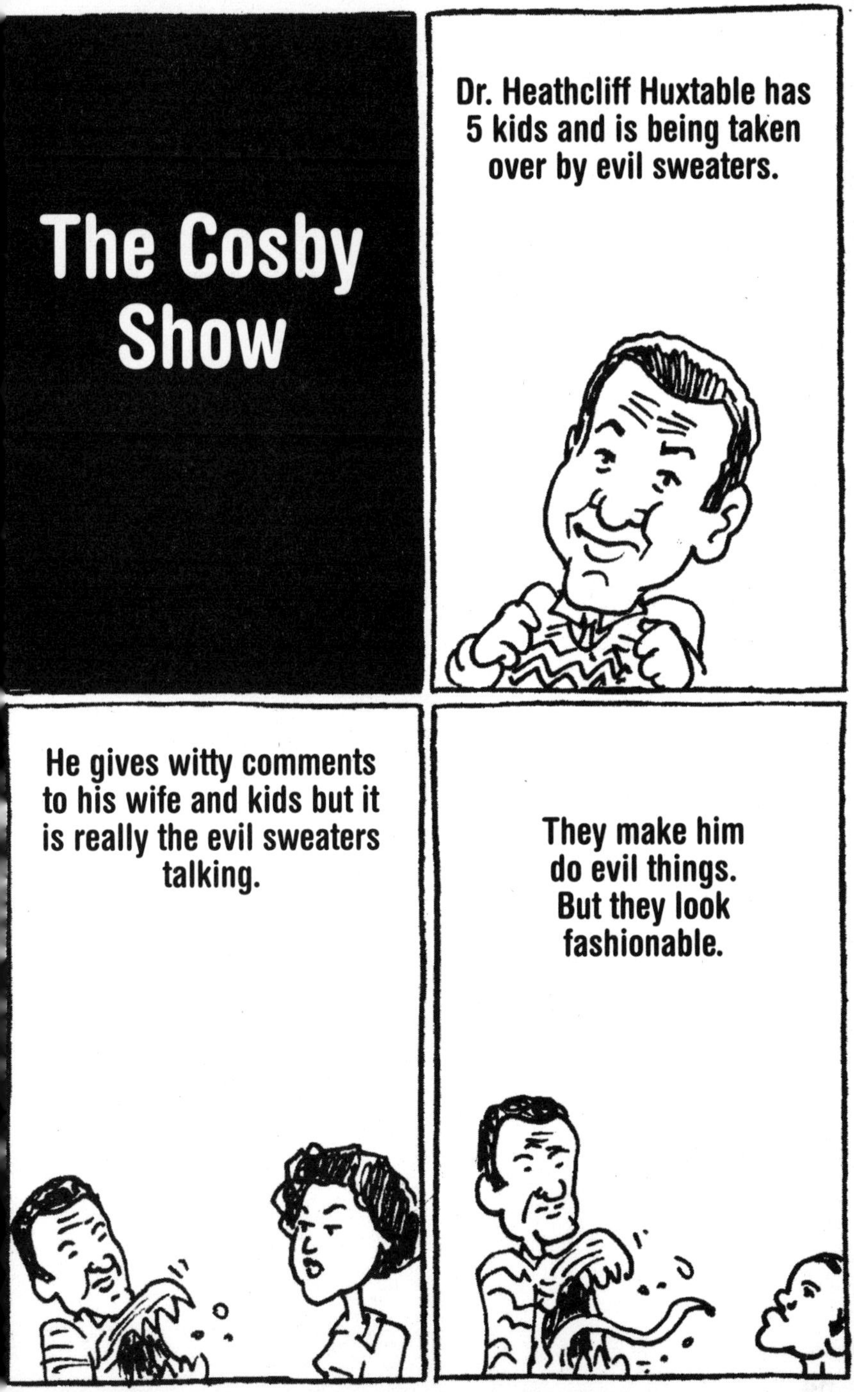
The Cosby Show
Dr. Heathcliff Huxtable has 5 kids and is being taken over by evil sweaters.
He gives witty comments to his wife and kids but it is really the evil sweaters talking.
They make him do evil things. But they look fashionable.

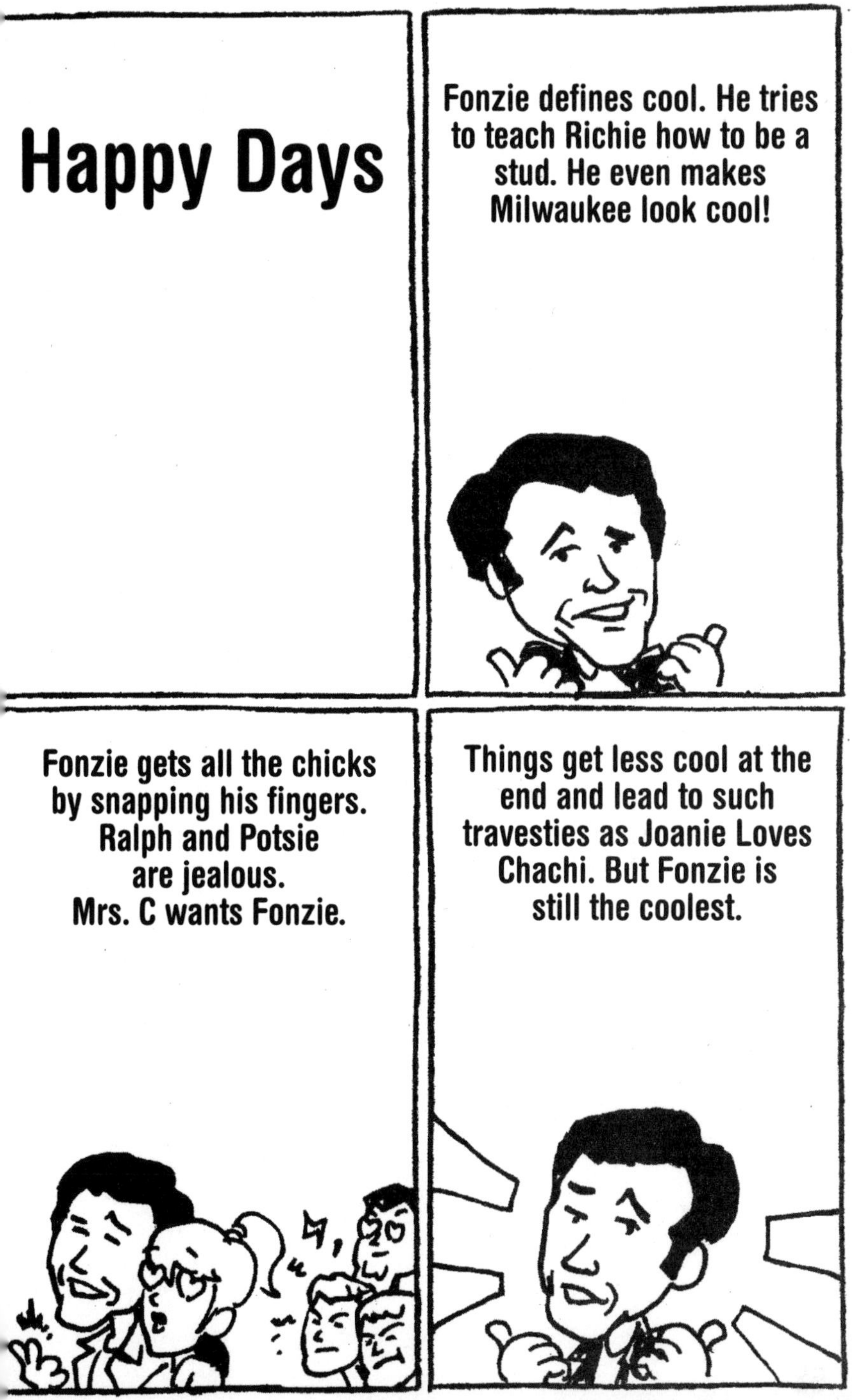
Happy Days
Fonzie defines cool. He tries to teach Richie how to be a stud. He even makes Milwaukee look cool!
Fonzie gets all the chicks by snapping his fingers. Ralph and Potsie are jealous. Mrs. C wants Fonzie.
Things get less cool at the end and lead to such travesties as Joanie Loves Chachi. But Fonzie is still the coolest.

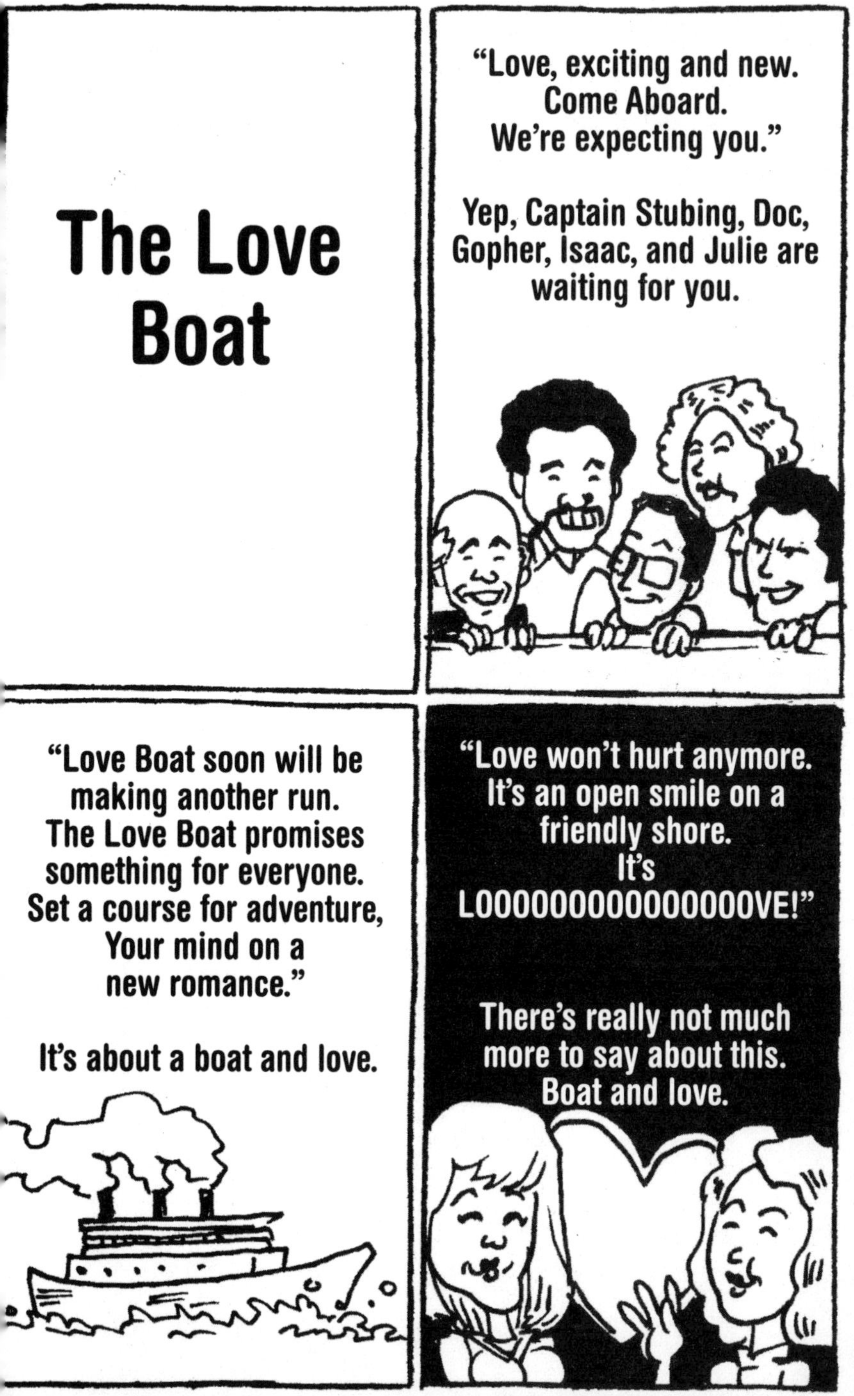
The Love Boat
"Love, exciting and new.
Come Aboard.
We're expecting you."
Yep, Captain Stubing, Doc, Gopher, Isaac, and Julie are waiting for you.
"Love Boat soon will be making another run.
The Love Boat promises something for everyone.
Set a course for adventure,
Your mind on a new romance."
It's about a boat and love.
"Love won't hurt anymore.
It's an open smile on a friendly shore.
It's
LOOOOOOOOOOOOOOOVE!"
There's really not much more to say about this.
Boat and love.

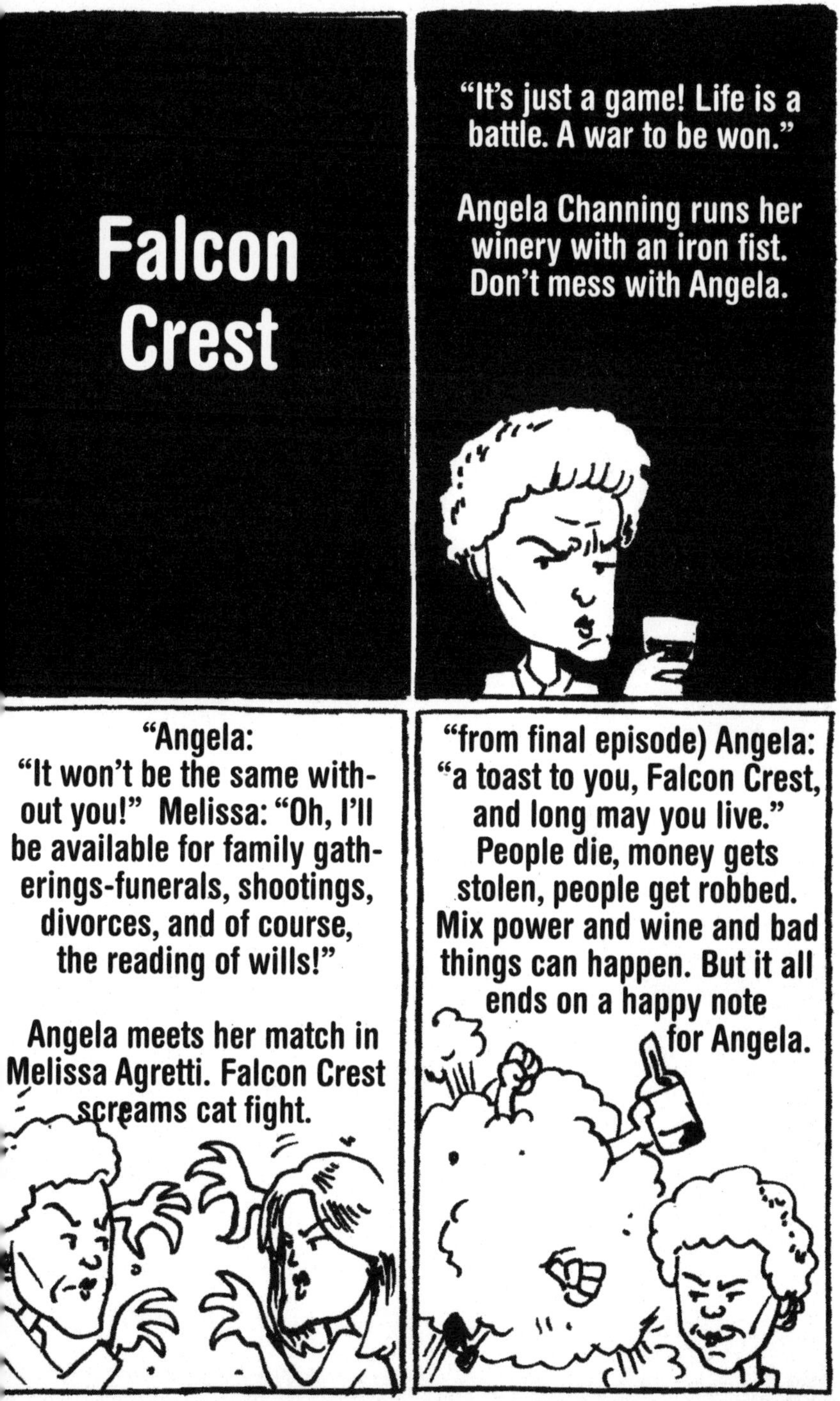
Falcon Crest
“It’s just a game! Life is a battle. A war to be won.”
Angela Channing runs her winery with an iron fist. Don’t mess with Angela.
“Angela: “It won’t be the same without you!” Melissa: “Oh, I’ll be available for family gatherings-funerals, shootings, divorces, and of course, the reading of wills!”
Angela meets her match in Melissa Agretti. Falcon Crest screams cat fight.
“from final episode) Angela: “a toast to you, Falcon Crest, and long may you live.” People die, money gets stolen, people get robbed. Mix power and wine and bad things can happen. But it all ends on a happy note for Angela.

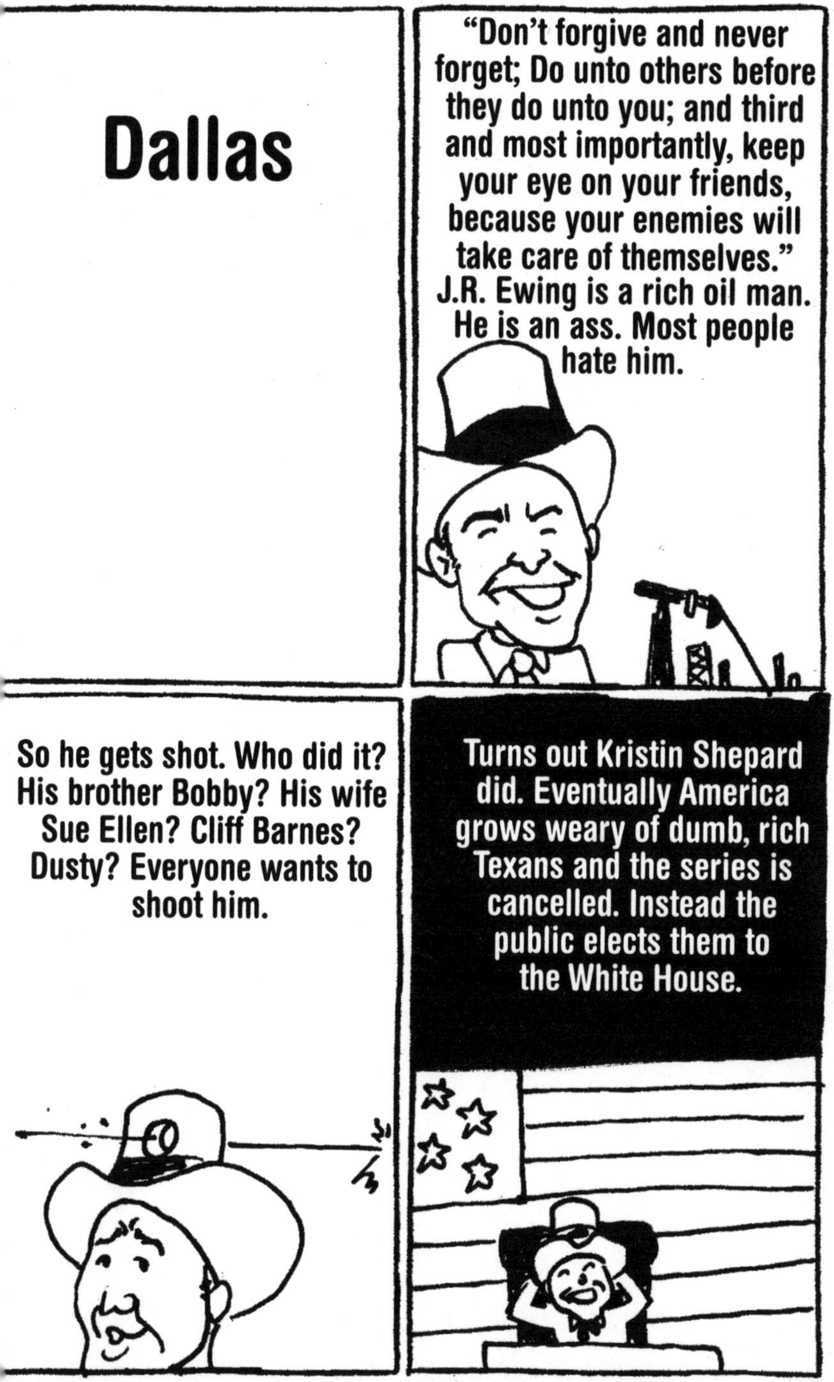
Dallas
"Don't forgive and never forget; Do unto others before they do unto you; and third and most importantly, keep your eye on your friends, because your enemies will take care of themselves." J.R. Ewing is a rich oil man. He is an ass. Most people hate him.
So he gets shot. Who did it? His brother Bobby? His wife Sue Ellen? Cliff Barnes? Dusty? Everyone wants to shoot him.
Turns out Kristin Shepard did. Eventually America grows weary of dumb, rich Texans and the series is cancelled. Instead the public elects them to the White House.

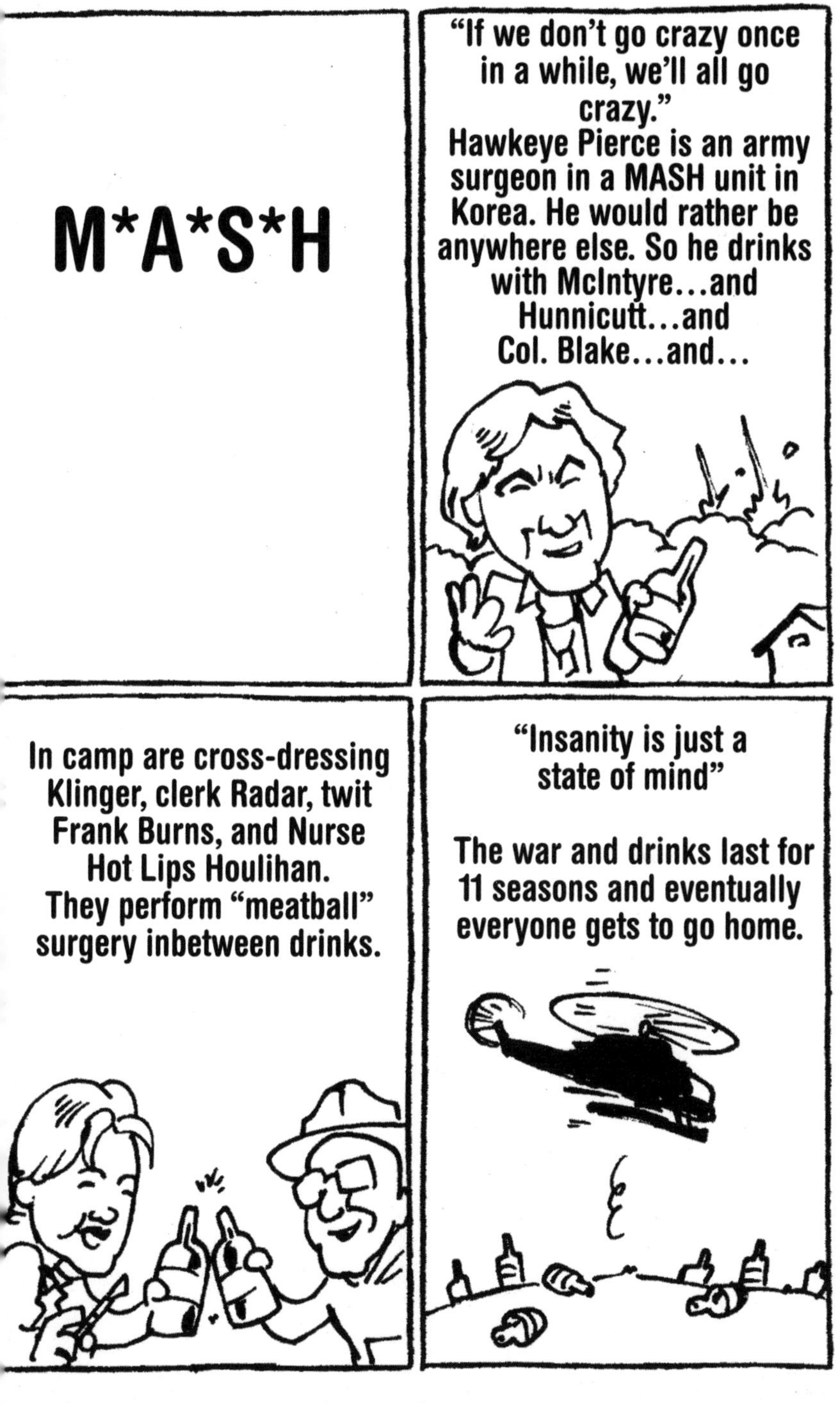
M*A*S*H
"If we don't go crazy once in a while, we'll all go crazy."
Hawkeye Pierce is an army surgeon in a MASH unit in Korea. He would rather be anywhere else. So he drinks with McIntyre…and Hunnicutt…and Col. Blake…and…
In camp are cross-dressing Klinger, clerk Radar, twit Frank Burns, and Nurse Hot Lips Houlihan. They perform "meatball" surgery inbetween drinks.
"Insanity is just a state of mind"
The war and drinks last for 11 seasons and eventually everyone gets to go home.

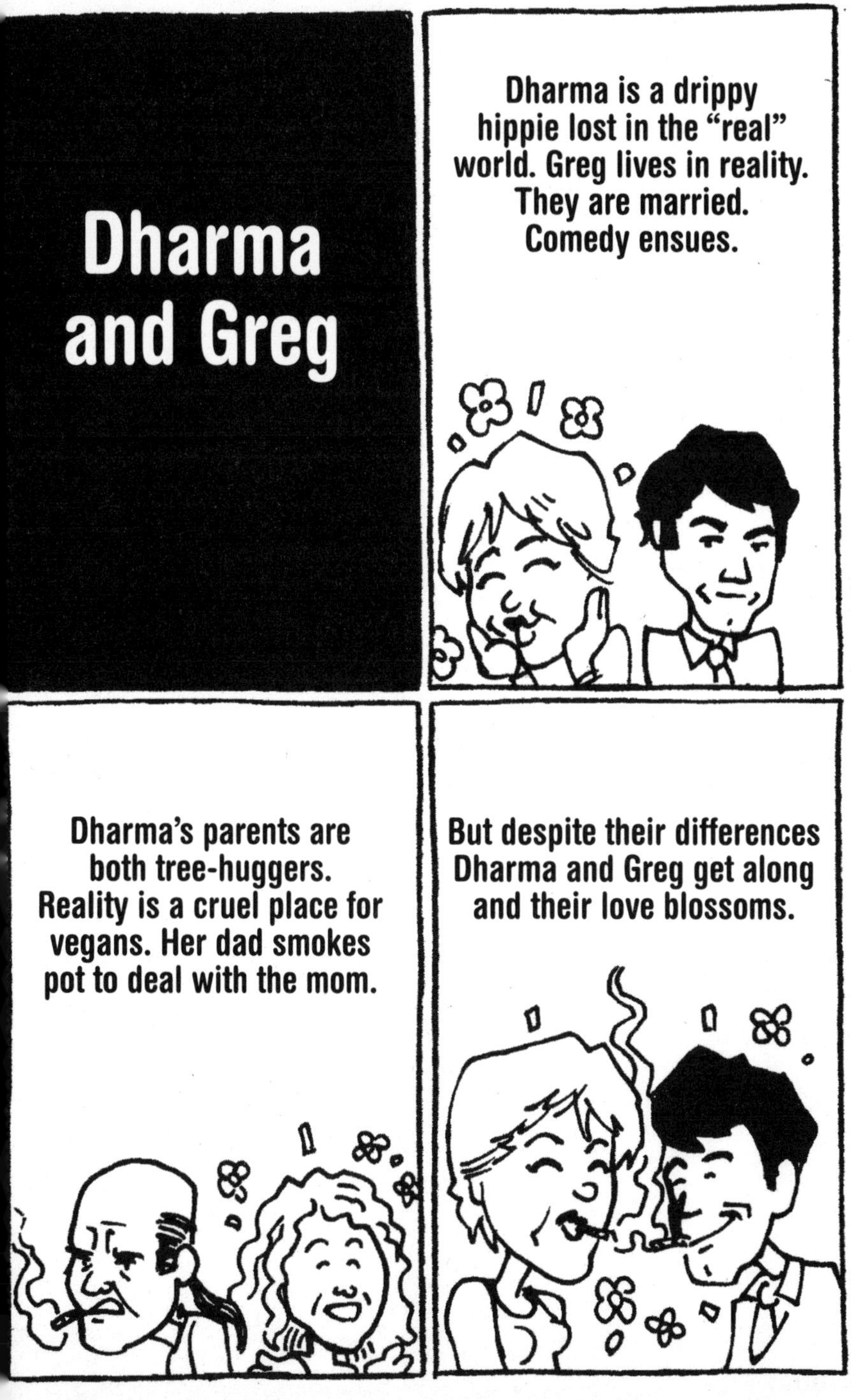
Dharma and Greg
Dharma is a drippy hippie lost in the "real" world. Greg lives in reality. They are married. Comedy ensues.
Dharma's parents are both tree-huggers. Reality is a cruel place for vegans. Her dad smokes pot to deal with the mom.
But despite their differences Dharma and Greg get along and their love blossoms.

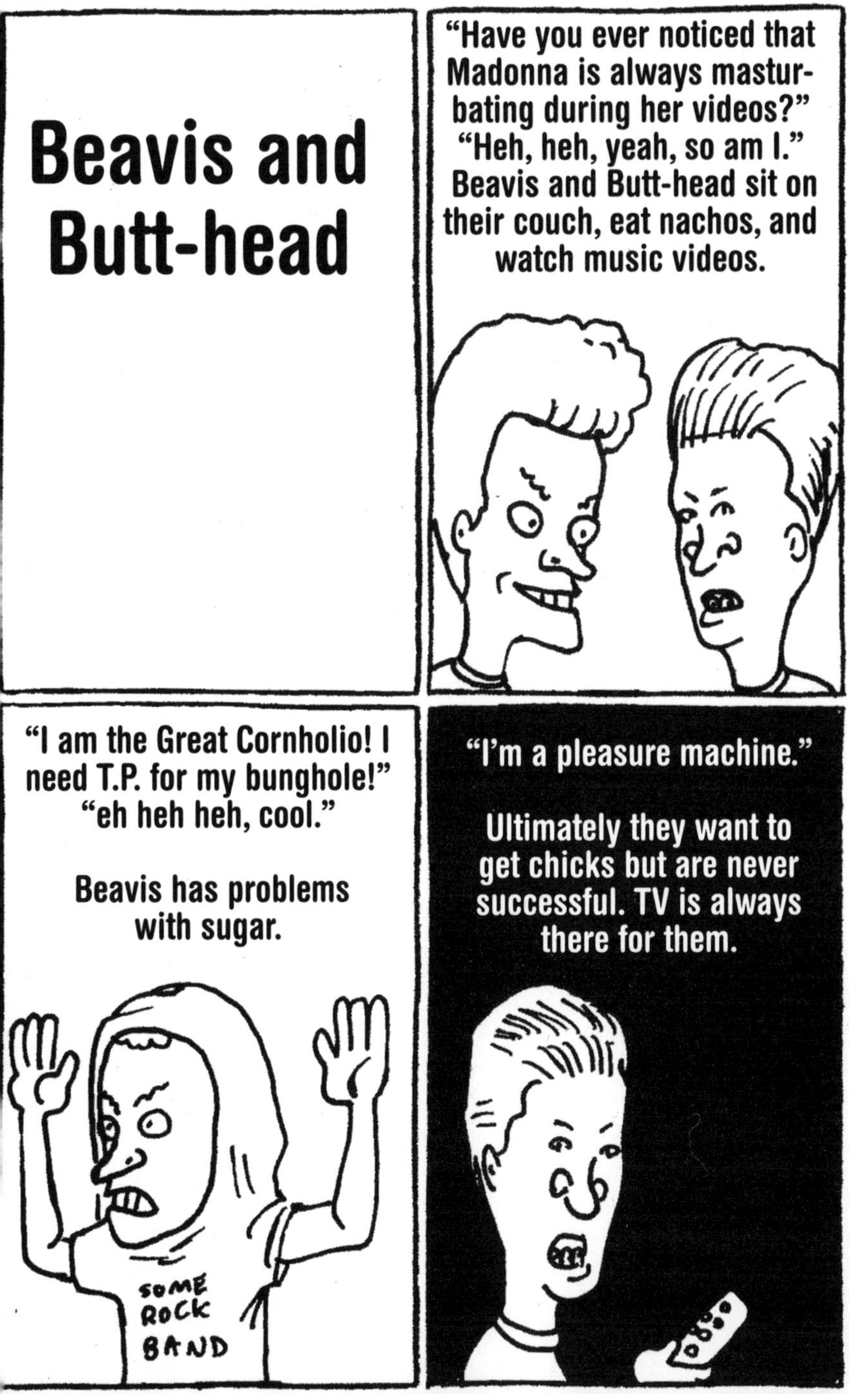
Beavis and Butt-head
"Have you ever noticed that Madonna is always masturbating during her videos?"
"Heh, heh, yeah, so am I."
Beavis and Butt-head sit on their couch, eat nachos, and watch music videos.
"I am the Great Cornholio! I need T.P. for my bunghole!"
"eh heh heh, cool."
Beavis has problems with sugar.
SOME ROCK BAND
"I'm a pleasure machine."
Ultimately they want to get chicks but are never successful. TV is always there for them.

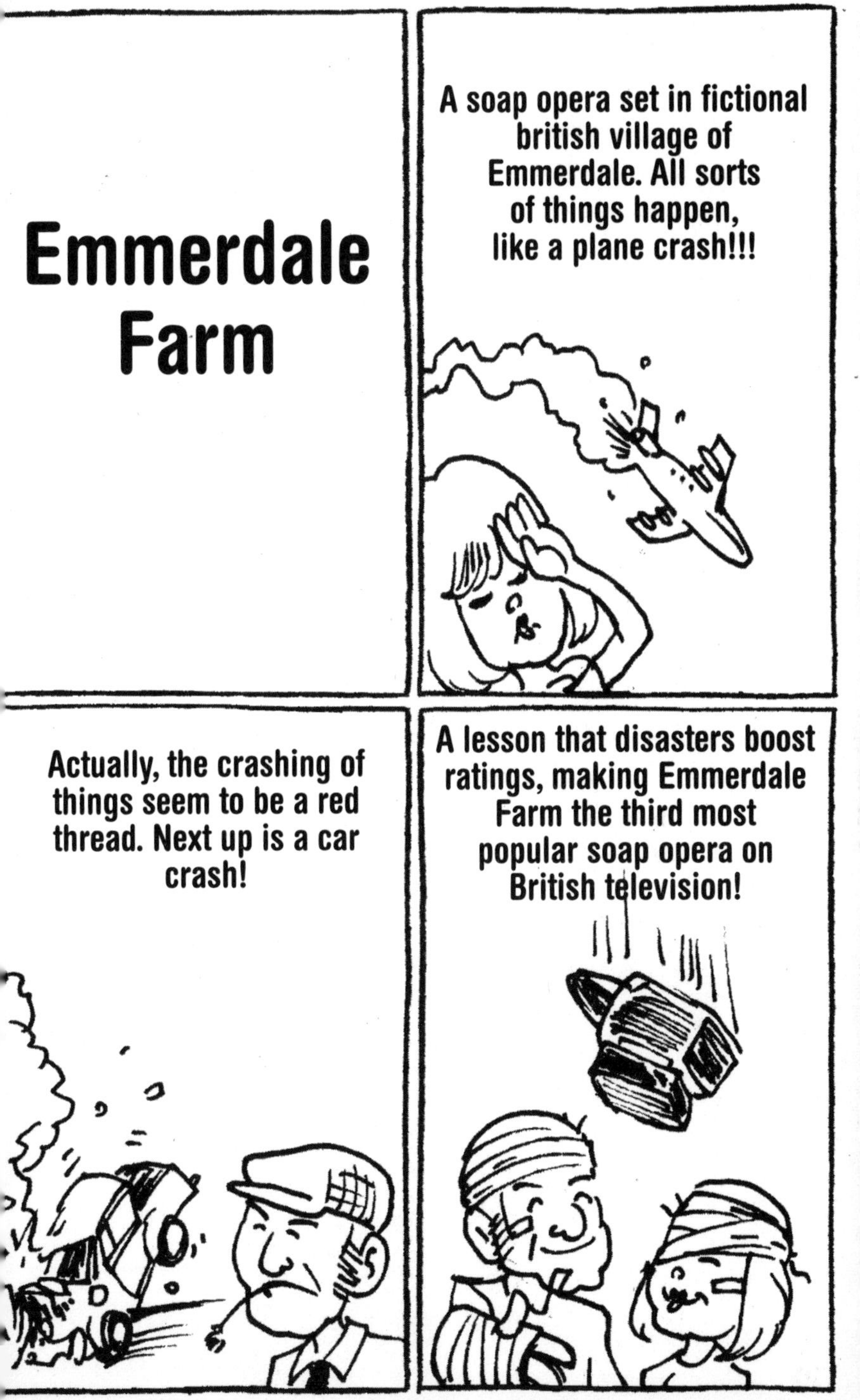
Emmerdale Farm
A soap opera set in fictional british village of Emmerdale. All sorts of things happen, like a plane crash!!!
Actually, the crashing of things seem to be a red thread. Next up is a car crash!
A lesson that disasters boost ratings, making Emmerdale Farm the third most popular soap opera on British television!

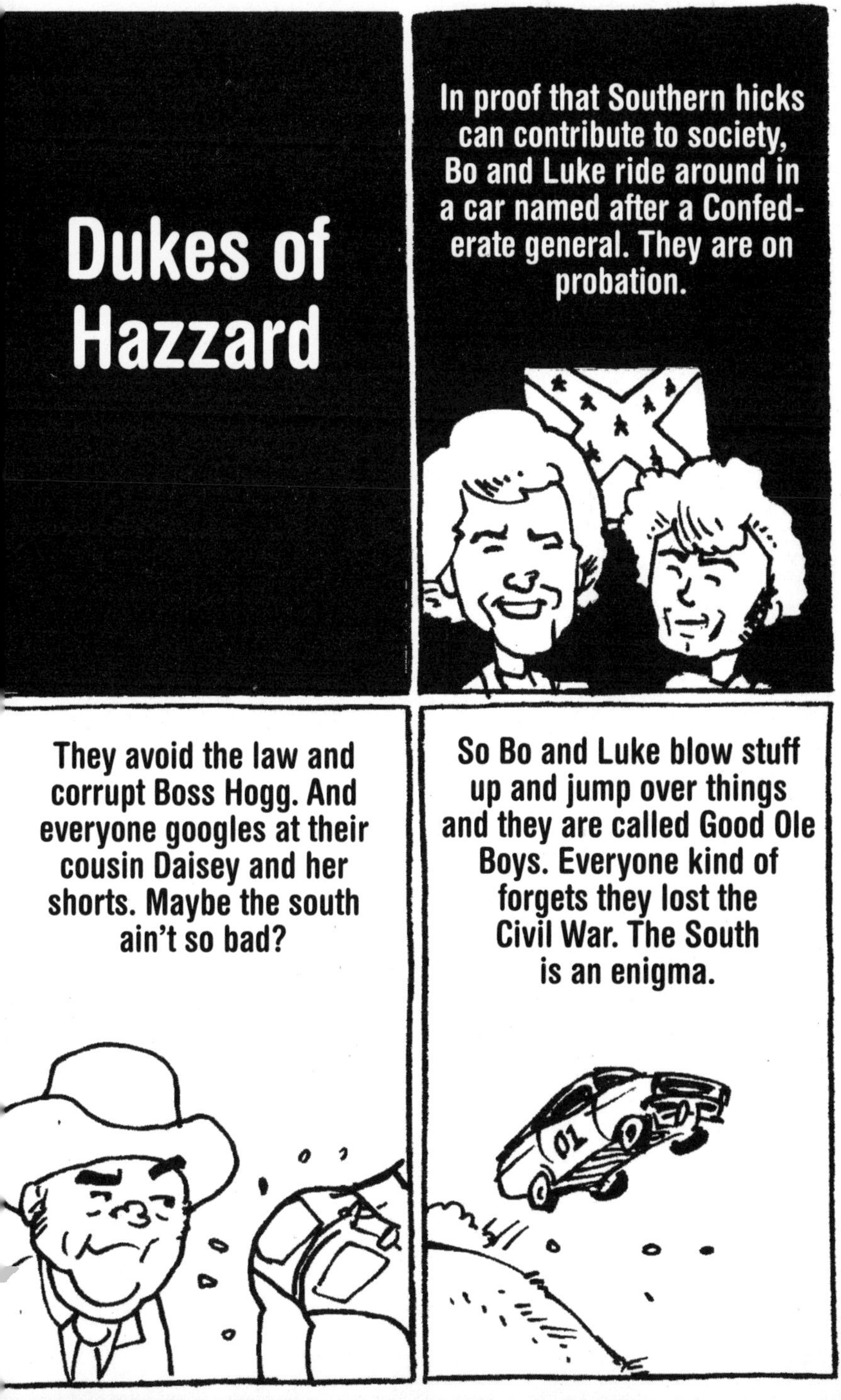
Dukes of Hazzard
In proof that Southern hicks can contribute to society, Bo and Luke ride around in a car named after a Confederate general. They are on probation.
They avoid the law and corrupt Boss Hogg. And everyone googles at their cousin Daisey and her shorts. Maybe the south ain't so bad?
So Bo and Luke blow stuff up and jump over things and they are called Good Ole Boys. Everyone kind of forgets they lost the Civil War. The South is an enigma.
01

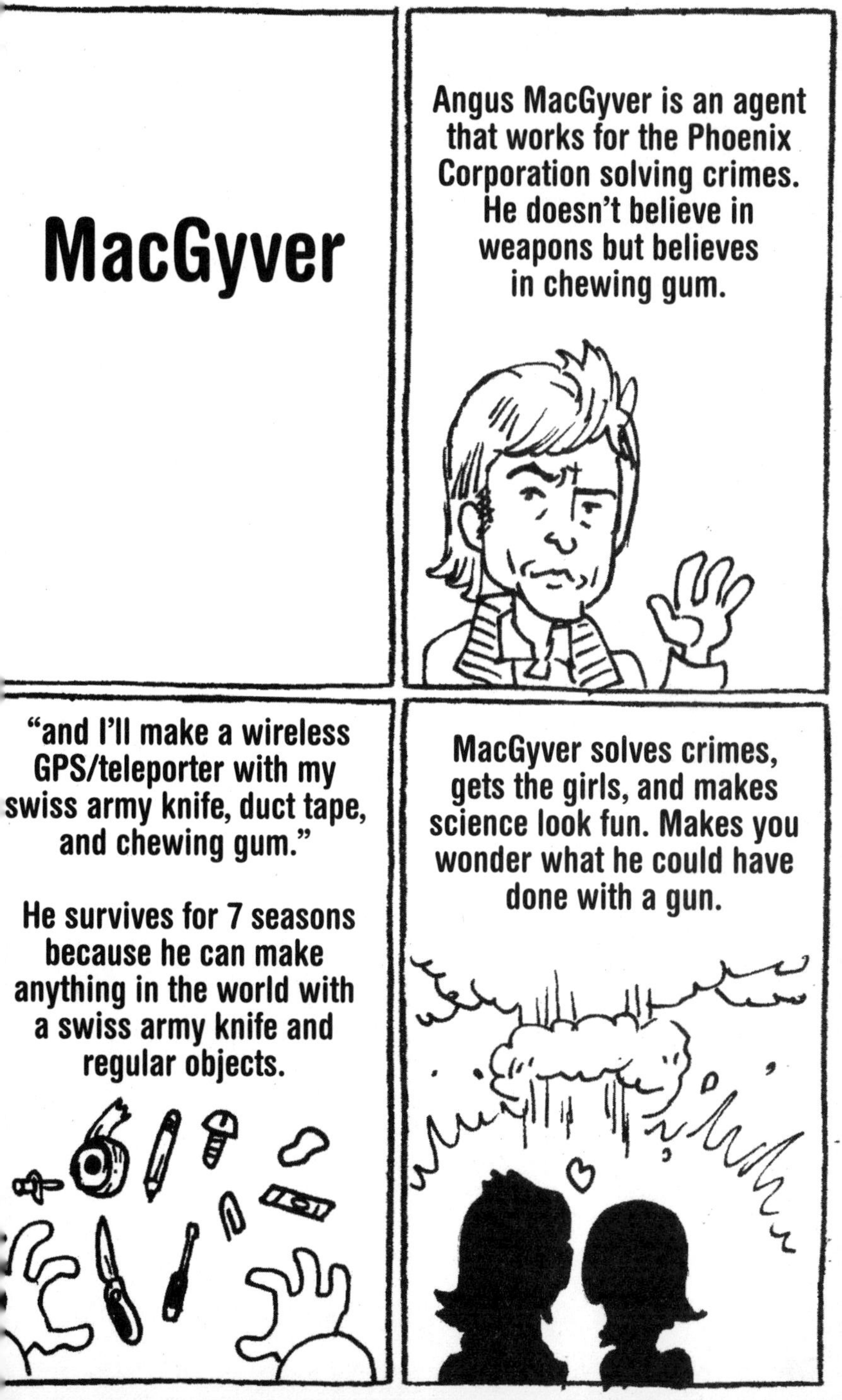
MacGyver
Angus MacGyver is an agent that works for the Phoenix Corporation solving crimes. He doesn't believe in weapons but believes in chewing gum.
"and I'll make a wireless GPS/teleporter with my swiss army knife, duct tape, and chewing gum."
He survives for 7 seasons because he can make anything in the world with a swiss army knife and regular objects.
MacGyver solves crimes, gets the girls, and makes science look fun. Makes you wonder what he could have done with a gun.

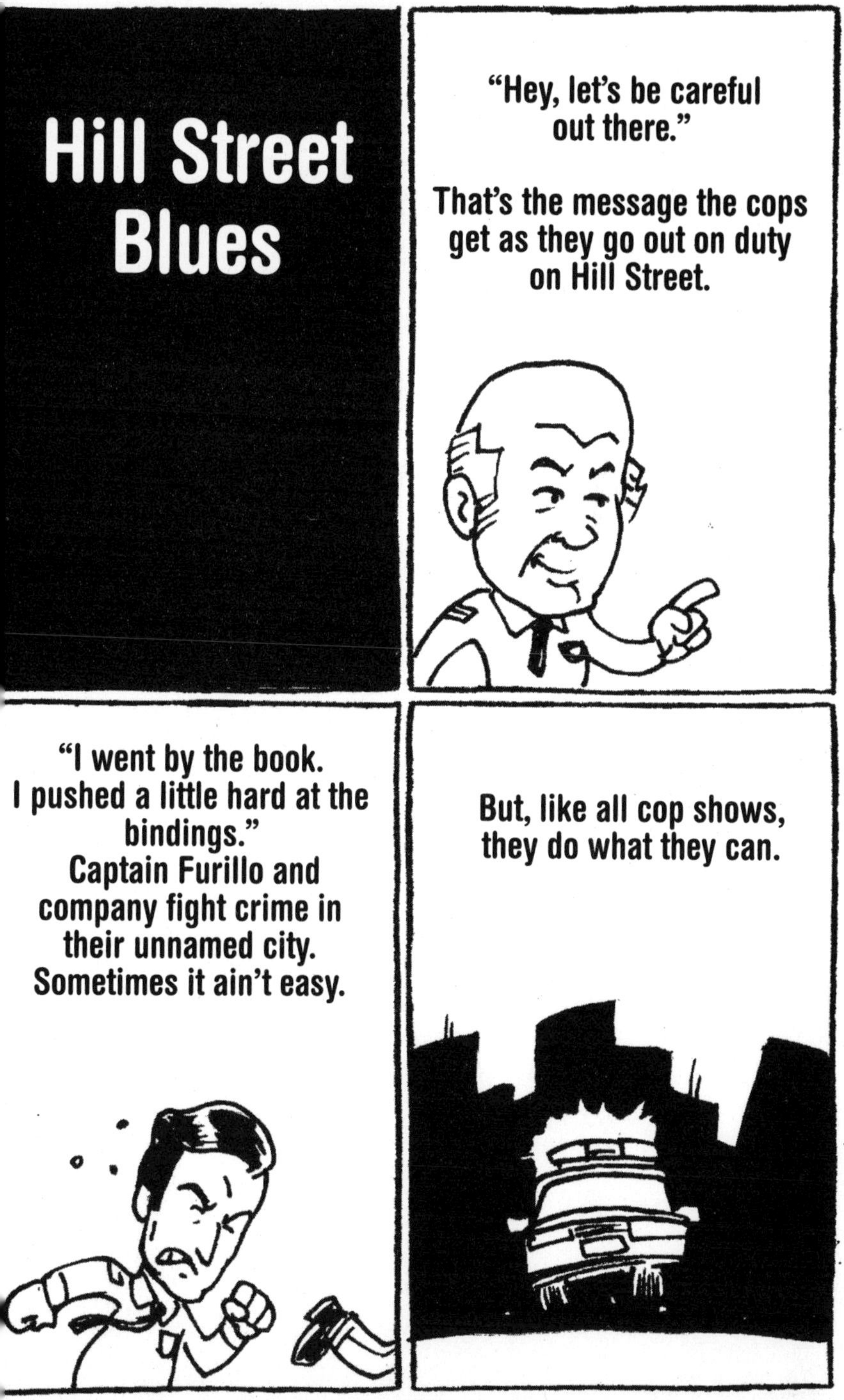
Hill Street Blues
"Hey, let's be careful out there."
That's the message the cops get as they go out on duty on Hill Street.
"I went by the book. I pushed a little hard at the bindings." Captain Furillo and company fight crime in their unnamed city. Sometimes it ain't easy.
But, like all cop shows, they do what they can.

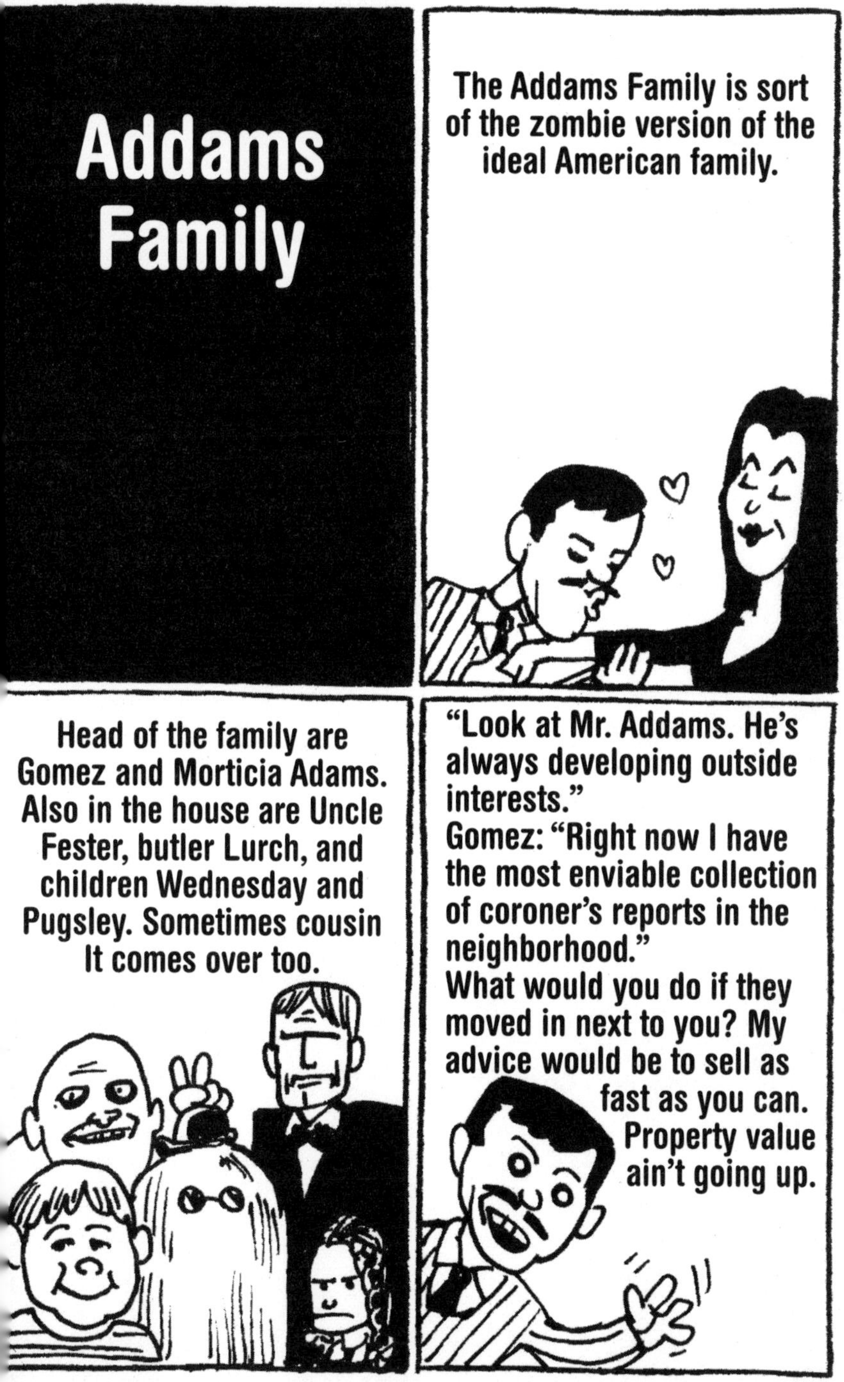
Addams Family
The Addams Family is sort of the zombie version of the ideal American family.
Head of the family are Gomez and Morticia Adams. Also in the house are Uncle Fester, butler Lurch, and children Wednesday and Pugsley. Sometimes cousin It comes over too.
"Look at Mr. Addams. He's always developing outside interests."
Gomez: "Right now I have the most enviable collection of coroner's reports in the neighborhood."
What would you do if they moved in next to you? My advice would be to sell as fast as you can. Property value ain't going up.

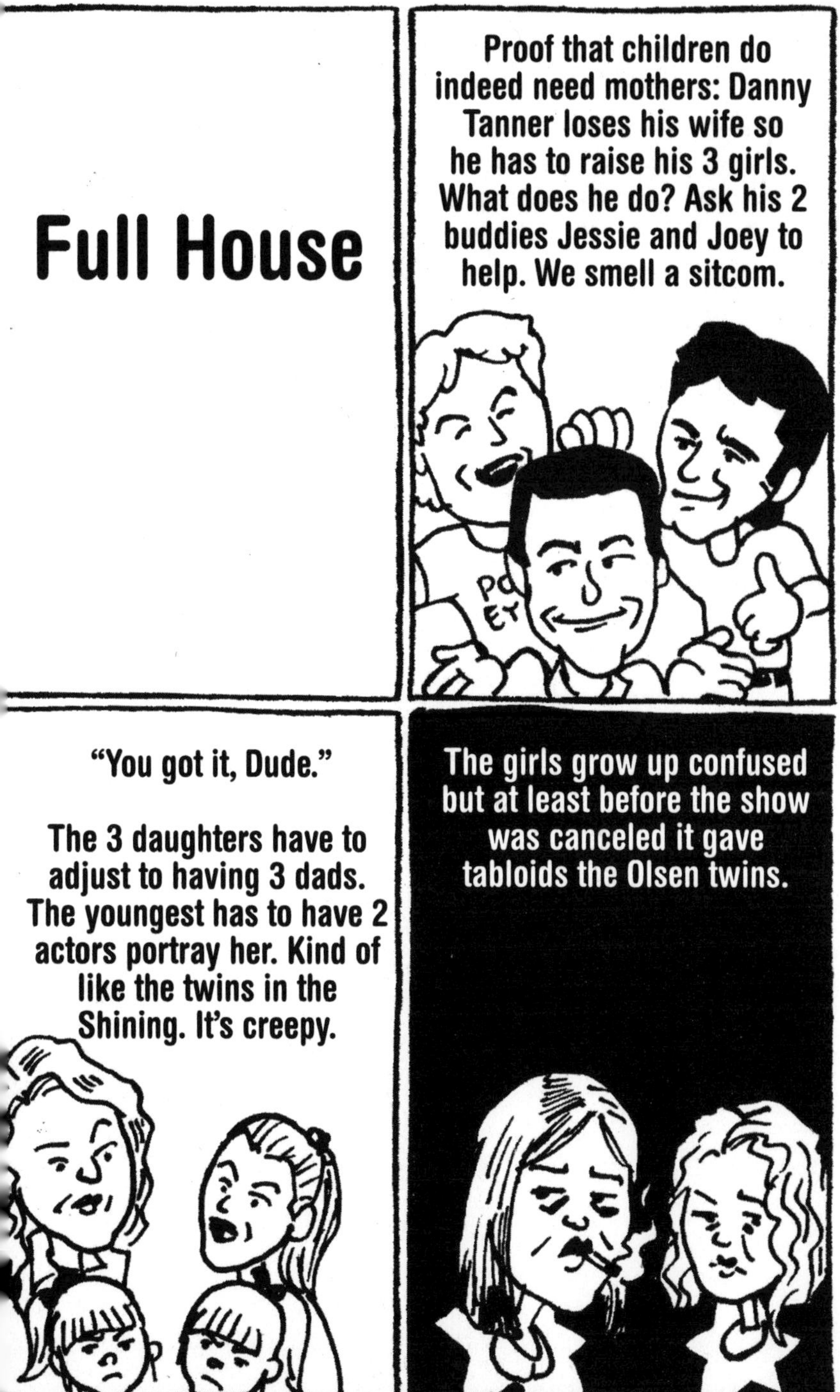
Full House
Proof that children do indeed need mothers: Danny Tanner loses his wife so he has to raise his 3 girls. What does he do? Ask his 2 buddies Jessie and Joey to help. We smell a sitcom.
"You got it, Dude."
The 3 daughters have to adjust to having 3 dads. The youngest has to have 2 actors portray her. Kind of like the twins in the Shining. It's creepy.
The girls grow up confused but at least before the show was canceled it gave tabloids the Olsen twins.

Home Improvement

"Some tool-men say: Why? This tool-man says: Why not?. Jill: This tool-man's wife says:Why me?".

Tim Taylor hosts the show "Tool Time" and lives with his wife and kids.

"Wilson, are you naked? Wilson: No, Tim, I am wearing a hat."

His Zen neighbor, Wilson, never shows his face. He is hiding something.

Tim's gets to build things and drive fast cars. His wife is very understanding. "My gynecologist just said Dr. Kaplan was the best urologist in town. How am I supposed to talk to a woman about what's going on in Manland? Now you got a theme park between your legs?)

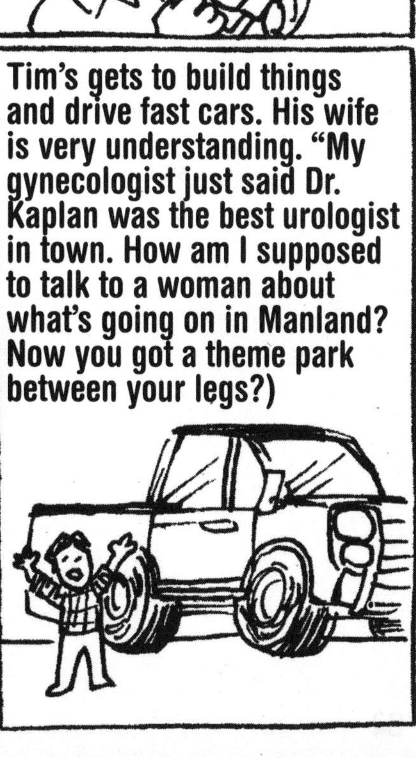

Married With Children

"I work in a shoe store, I make less than minimum wage, and yet I'm not happy to be home." White trash never looked so glorious as we see with the Bundy family. Al is a ladies shoe salesman always dreaming about his high school football days. Peggy is his wife who is lazier than Al. She likes to sit at home eating bon-bons.

"I want sex." Al: "So do I, but I see no reason to drag *you* into it."
Al and Peg rip on and appear to hate each other, but somehow managed to have 2 kids: Kelly and Bud.

Actually, everyone seems unhappy. So being white trash doesn't appear to have much upside. Even the dog is bitter.

Roseanne

"Here I am, 5 o'clock in the morning, stuffing breadcrumbs up a dead bird's butt."

Roseanne is a middle class woman that has a cynical view on life.

"You guys don't think we get your corny little sex jokes. You kids are our corny little sex jokes."

Her husband Dan and kids put up with her attitude.

"Now that I'm rich I don't have time to run other people's lifes." In the end she wins the lottery and everything turns out perfect... except it was just her dream. We thought they outlawed writers from dream write-offs. Guess not.

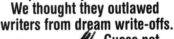

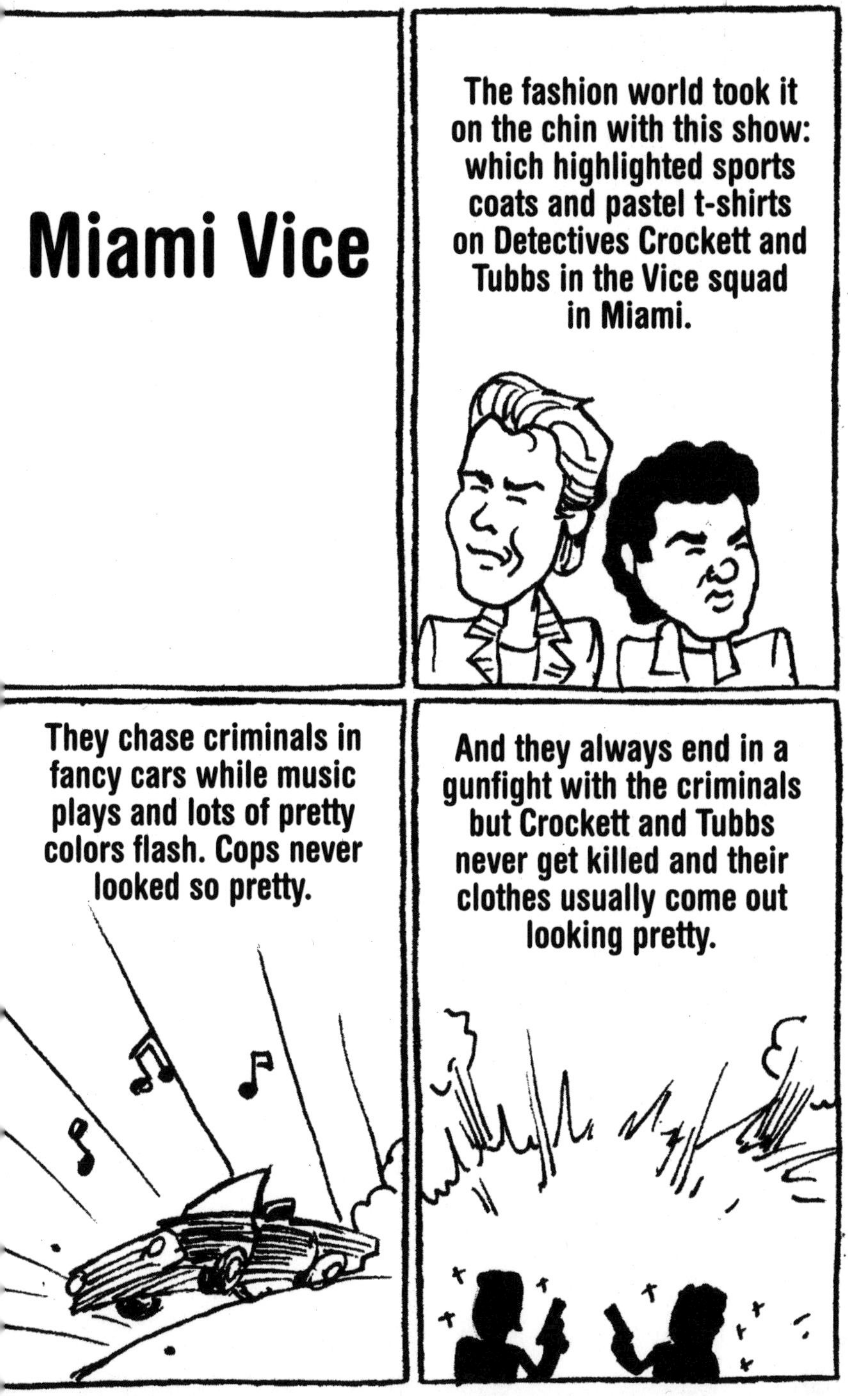
Miami Vice
The fashion world took it on the chin with this show: which highlighted sports coats and pastel t-shirts on Detectives Crockett and Tubbs in the Vice squad in Miami.
They chase criminals in fancy cars while music plays and lots of pretty colors flash. Cops never looked so pretty.
And they always end in a gunfight with the criminals but Crockett and Tubbs never get killed and their clothes usually come out looking pretty.

Family Ties

"People who have money don't need people." Alex Keaton is a good ole card carrying young Republican. His family resents his power.

His parents Steven and Elyse Keaton are trying to turn Alex into a liberal baby. But Alex is strong. He has the power of Reagan within him. His sisters Mallory and Jennifer are useless extras.

"Think what we're doing. We're taking a simple peasant girl and we're transforming her into somebody who could even have a conversation with me!" One day the whole family will see Alex's right wing points of view and the household will be a better place.

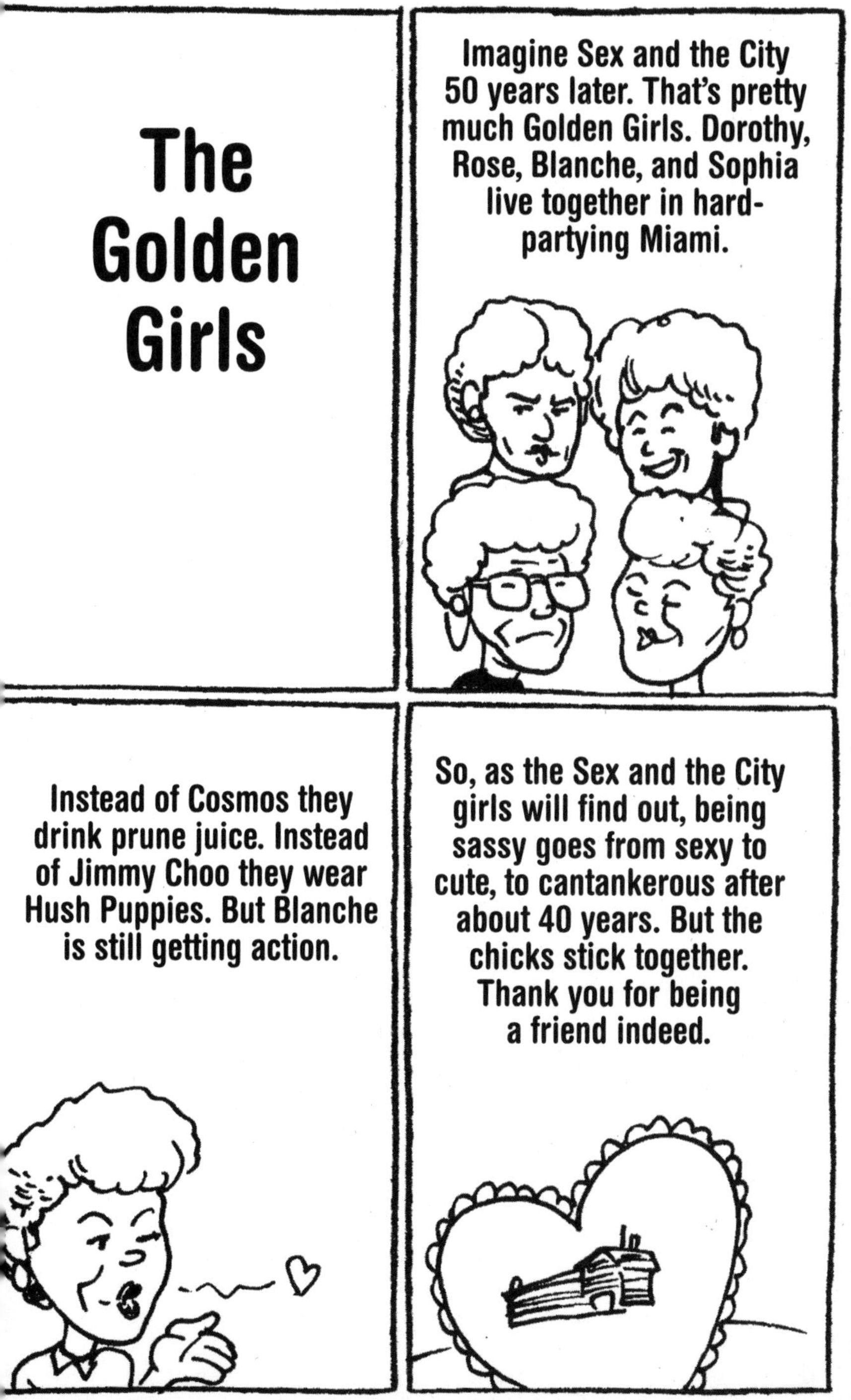
The Golden Girls
Imagine Sex and the City 50 years later. That's pretty much Golden Girls. Dorothy, Rose, Blanche, and Sophia live together in hard-partying Miami.
Instead of Cosmos they drink prune juice. Instead of Jimmy Choo they wear Hush Puppies. But Blanche is still getting action.
So, as the Sex and the City girls will find out, being sassy goes from sexy to cute, to cantankerous after about 40 years. But the chicks stick together. Thank you for being a friend indeed.

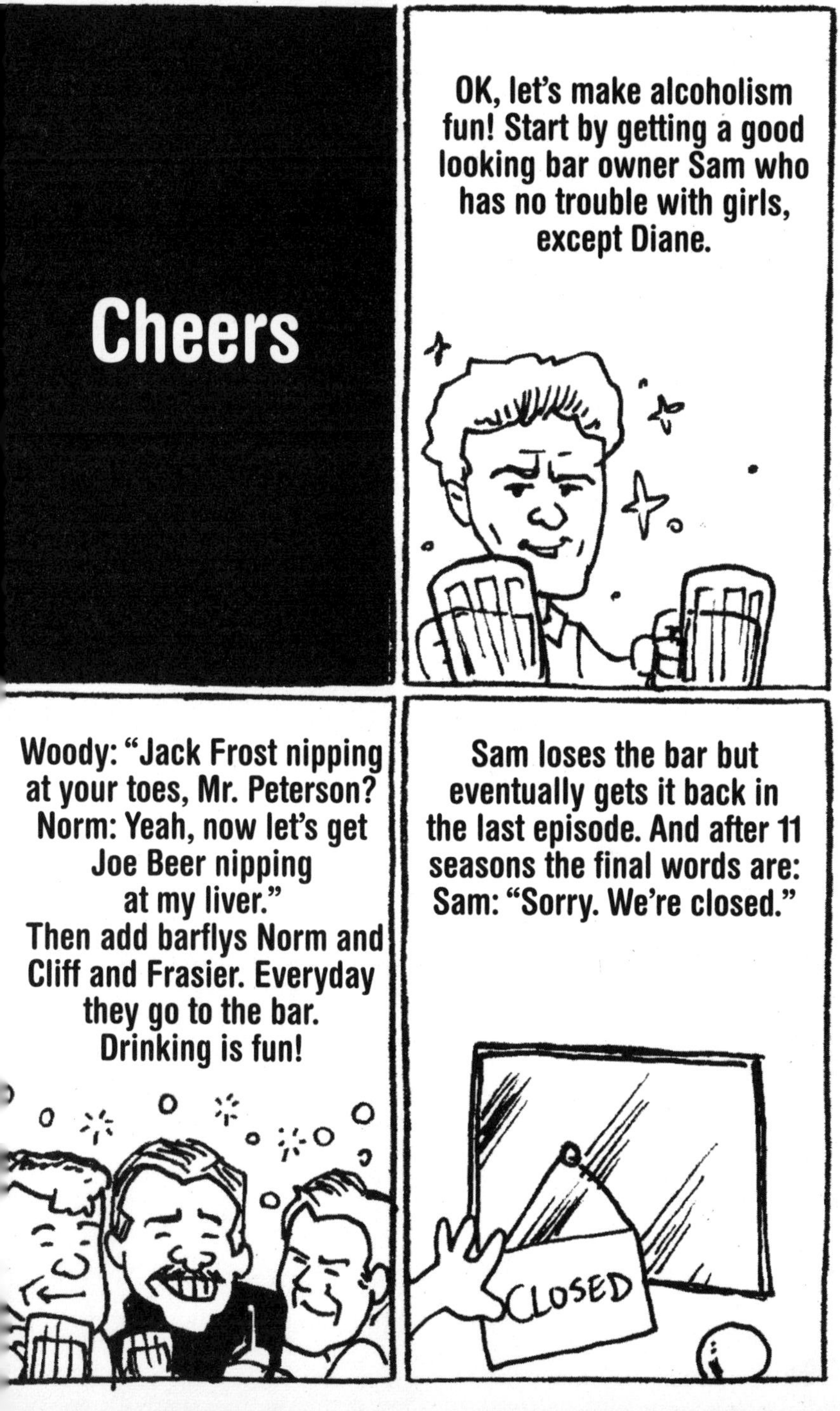
Cheers
OK, let's make alcoholism fun! Start by getting a good looking bar owner Sam who has no trouble with girls, except Diane.
Woody: "Jack Frost nipping at your toes, Mr. Peterson? Norm: Yeah, now let's get Joe Beer nipping at my liver."
Then add barflys Norm and Cliff and Frasier. Everyday they go to the bar. Drinking is fun!
Sam loses the bar but eventually gets it back in the last episode. And after 11 seasons the final words are: Sam: "Sorry. We're closed."
CLOSED

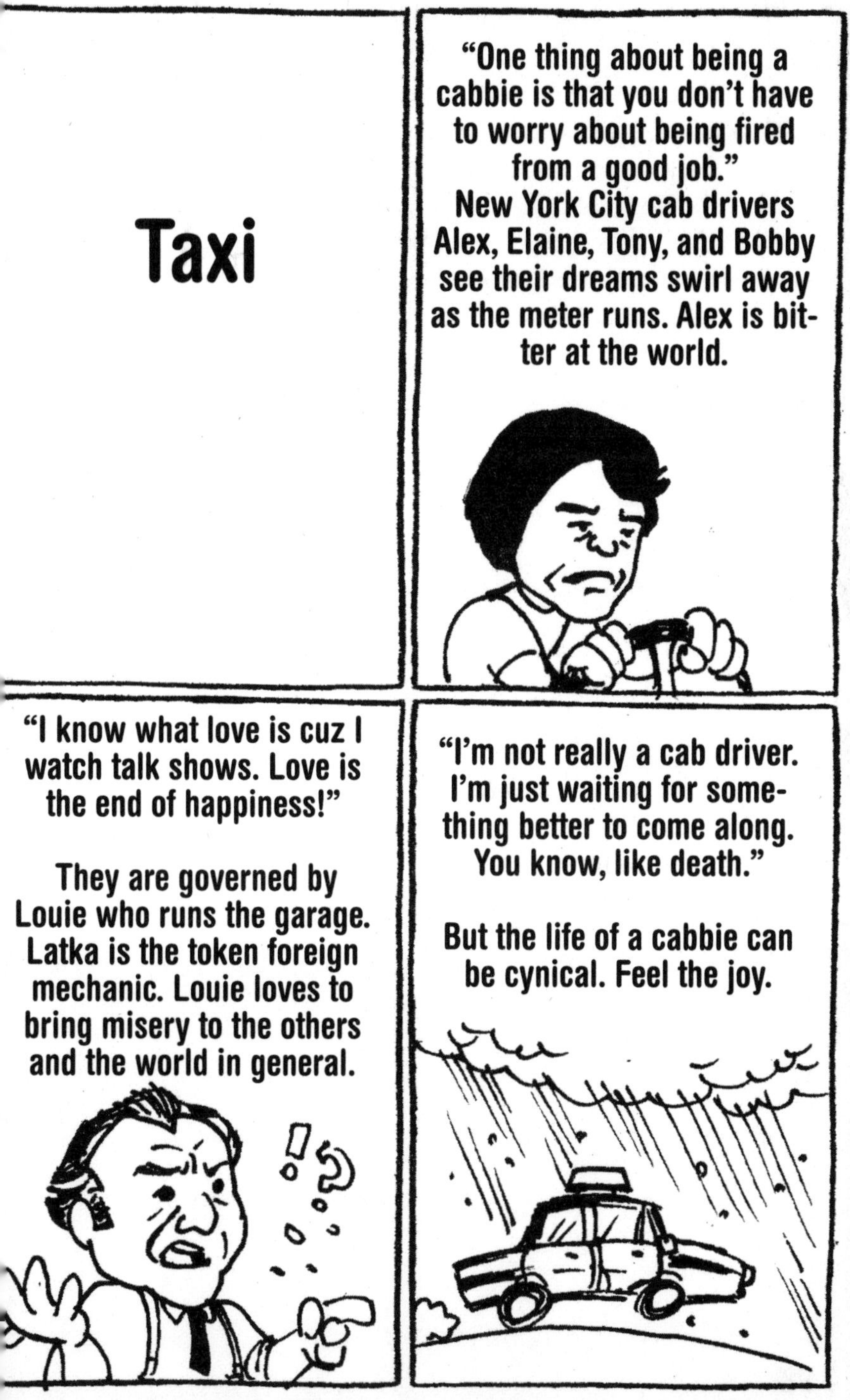
Taxi
"One thing about being a cabbie is that you don't have to worry about being fired from a good job."
New York City cab drivers Alex, Elaine, Tony, and Bobby see their dreams swirl away as the meter runs. Alex is bitter at the world.
"I know what love is cuz I watch talk shows. Love is the end of happiness!"
They are governed by Louie who runs the garage. Latka is the token foreign mechanic. Louie loves to bring misery to the others and the world in general.
"I'm not really a cab driver. I'm just waiting for something better to come along. You know, like death."
But the life of a cabbie can be cynical. Feel the joy.

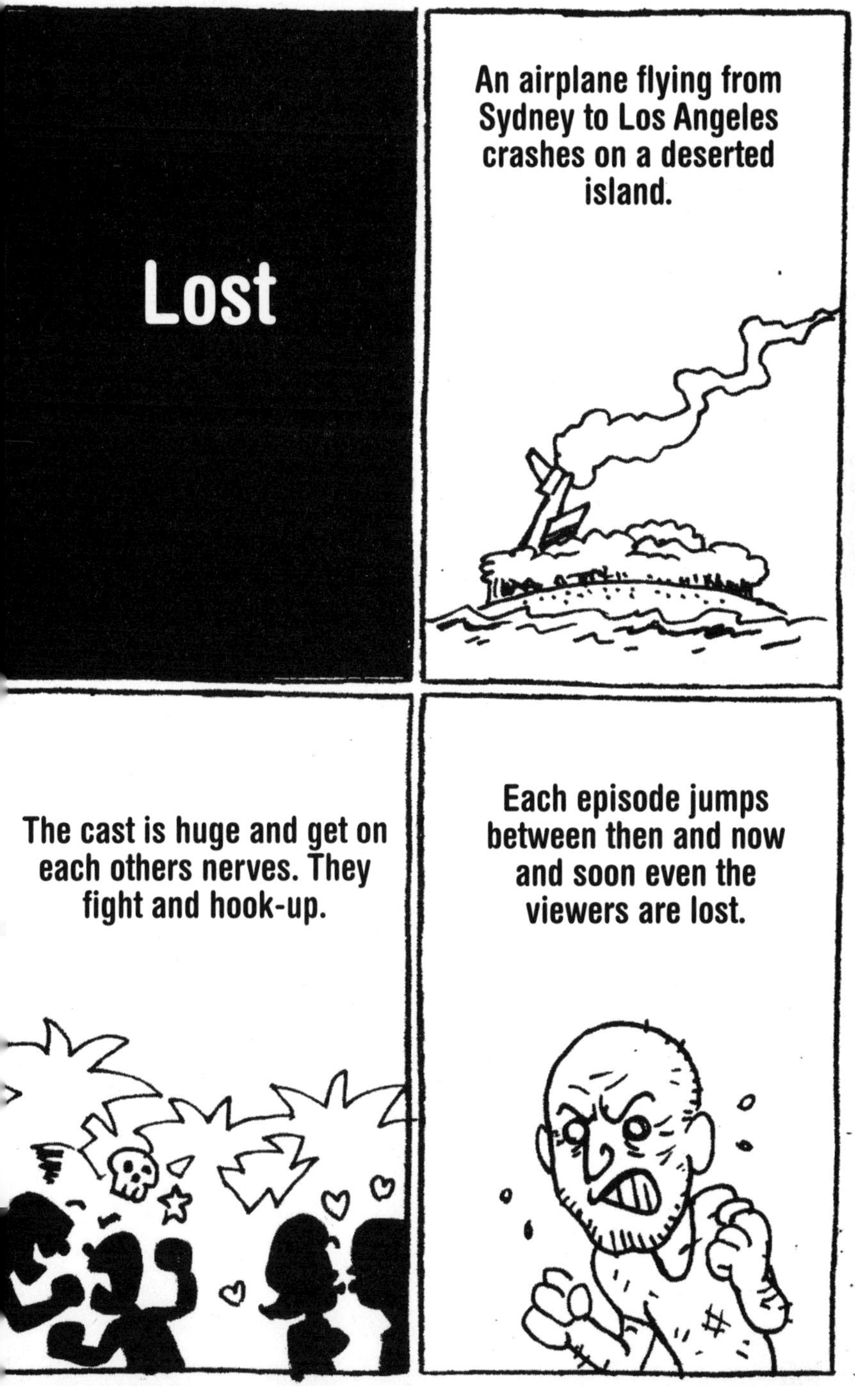
Lost
An airplane flying from Sydney to Los Angeles crashes on a deserted island.
The cast is huge and get on each others nerves. They fight and hook-up.
Each episode jumps between then and now and soon even the viewers are lost.

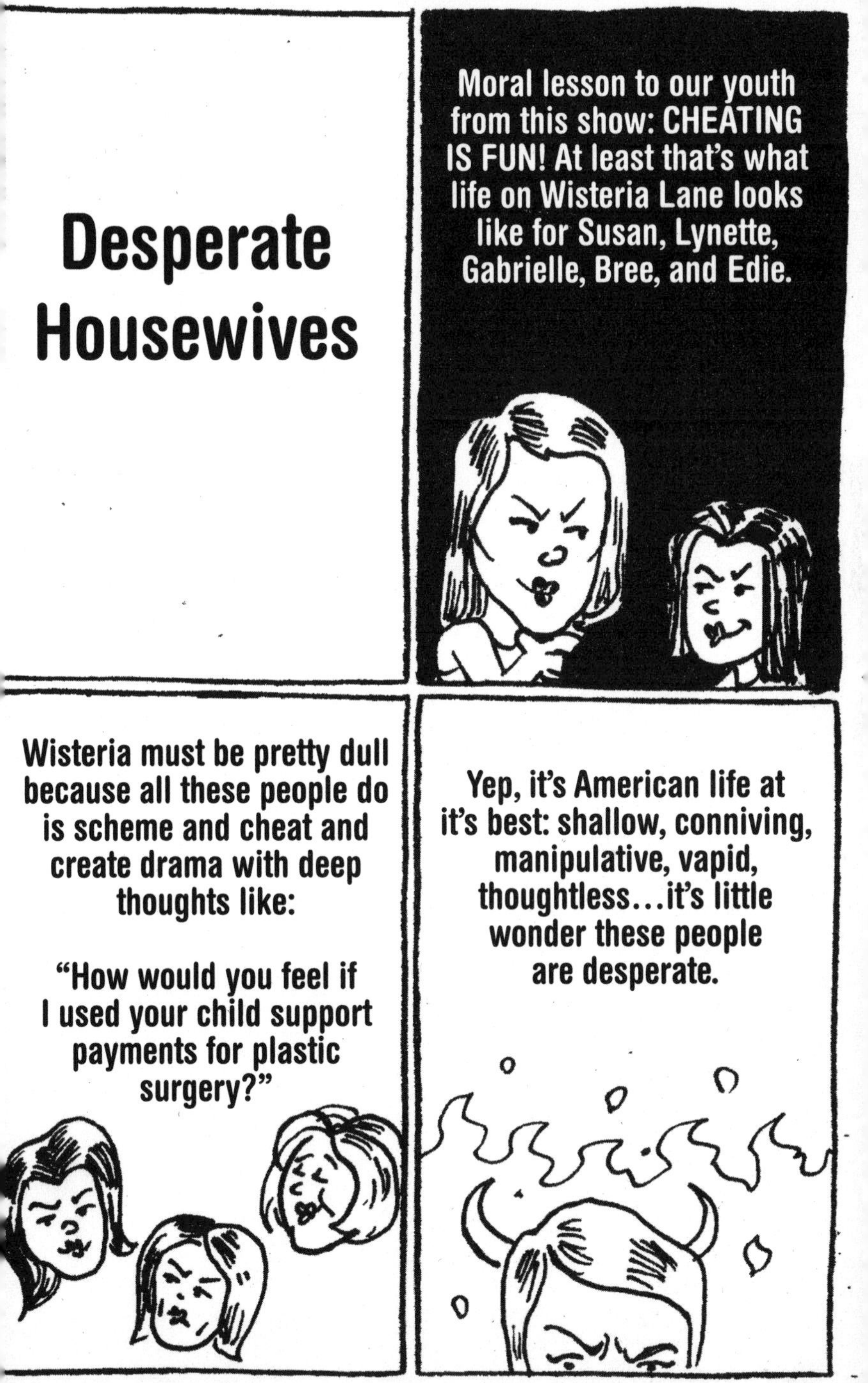
Desperate Housewives
Moral lesson to our youth from this show: CHEATING IS FUN! At least that's what life on Wisteria Lane looks like for Susan, Lynette, Gabrielle, Bree, and Edie.
Wisteria must be pretty dull because all these people do is scheme and cheat and create drama with deep thoughts like:
"How would you feel if I used your child support payments for plastic surgery?"
Yep, it's American life at it's best: shallow, conniving, manipulative, vapid, thoughtless...it's little wonder these people are desperate.

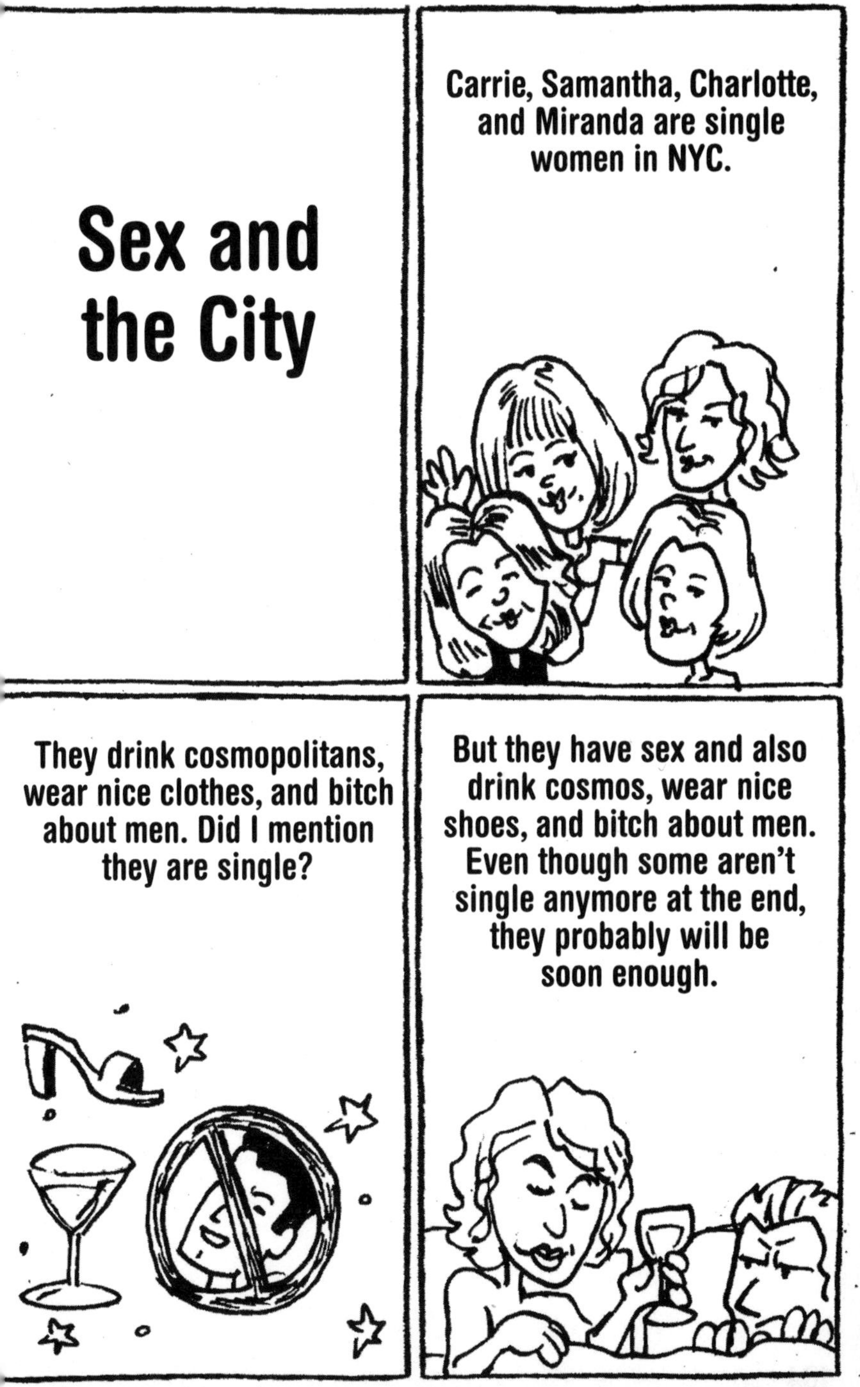
Sex and the City
Carrie, Samantha, Charlotte, and Miranda are single women in NYC.
They drink cosmopolitans, wear nice clothes, and bitch about men. Did I mention they are single?
But they have sex and also drink cosmos, wear nice shoes, and bitch about men. Even though some aren't single anymore at the end, they probably will be soon enough.

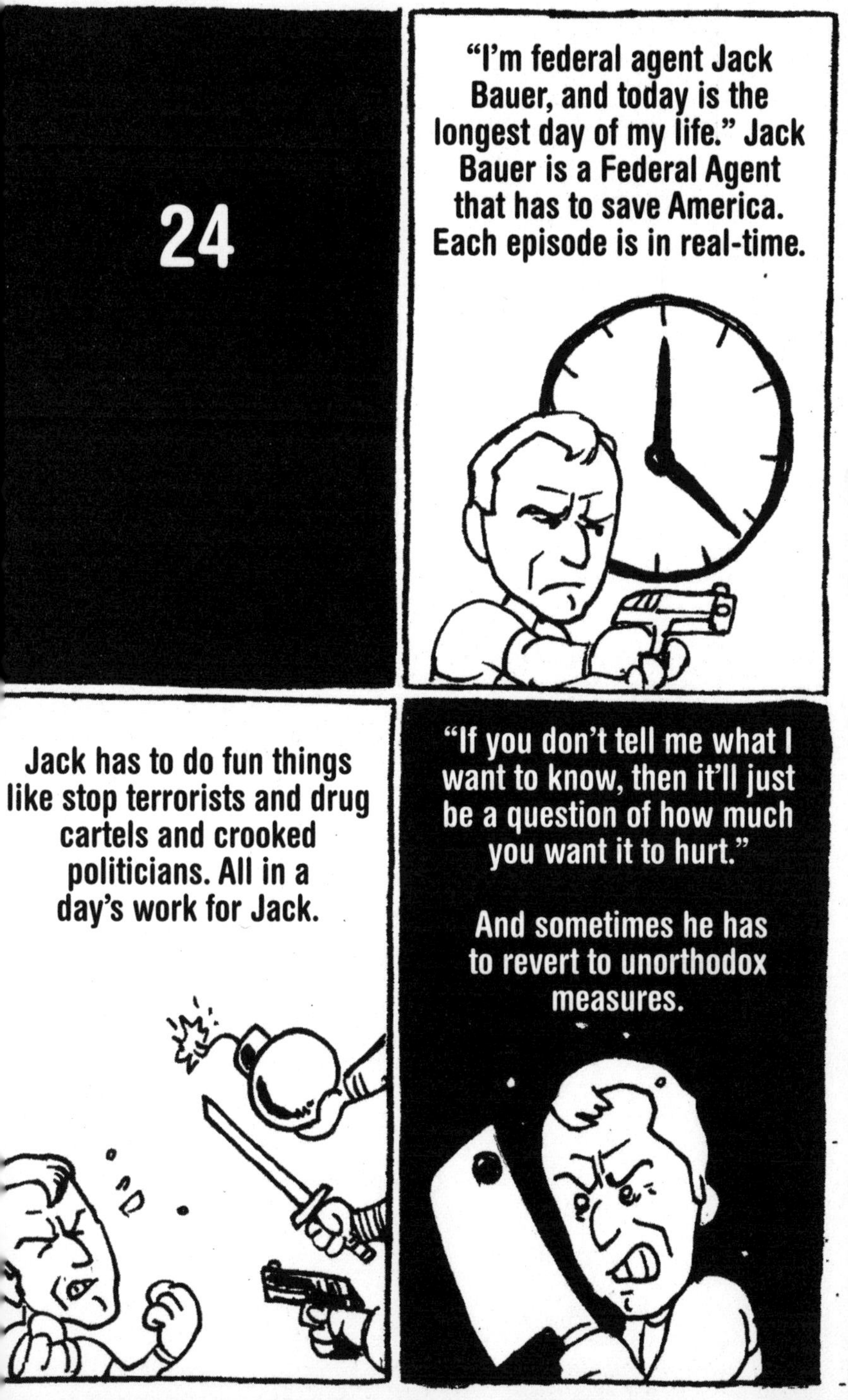
24
"I'm federal agent Jack Bauer, and today is the longest day of my life." Jack Bauer is a Federal Agent that has to save America. Each episode is in real-time.
Jack has to do fun things like stop terrorists and drug cartels and crooked politicians. All in a day's work for Jack.
"If you don't tell me what I want to know, then it'll just be a question of how much you want it to hurt."
And sometimes he has to revert to unorthodox measures.

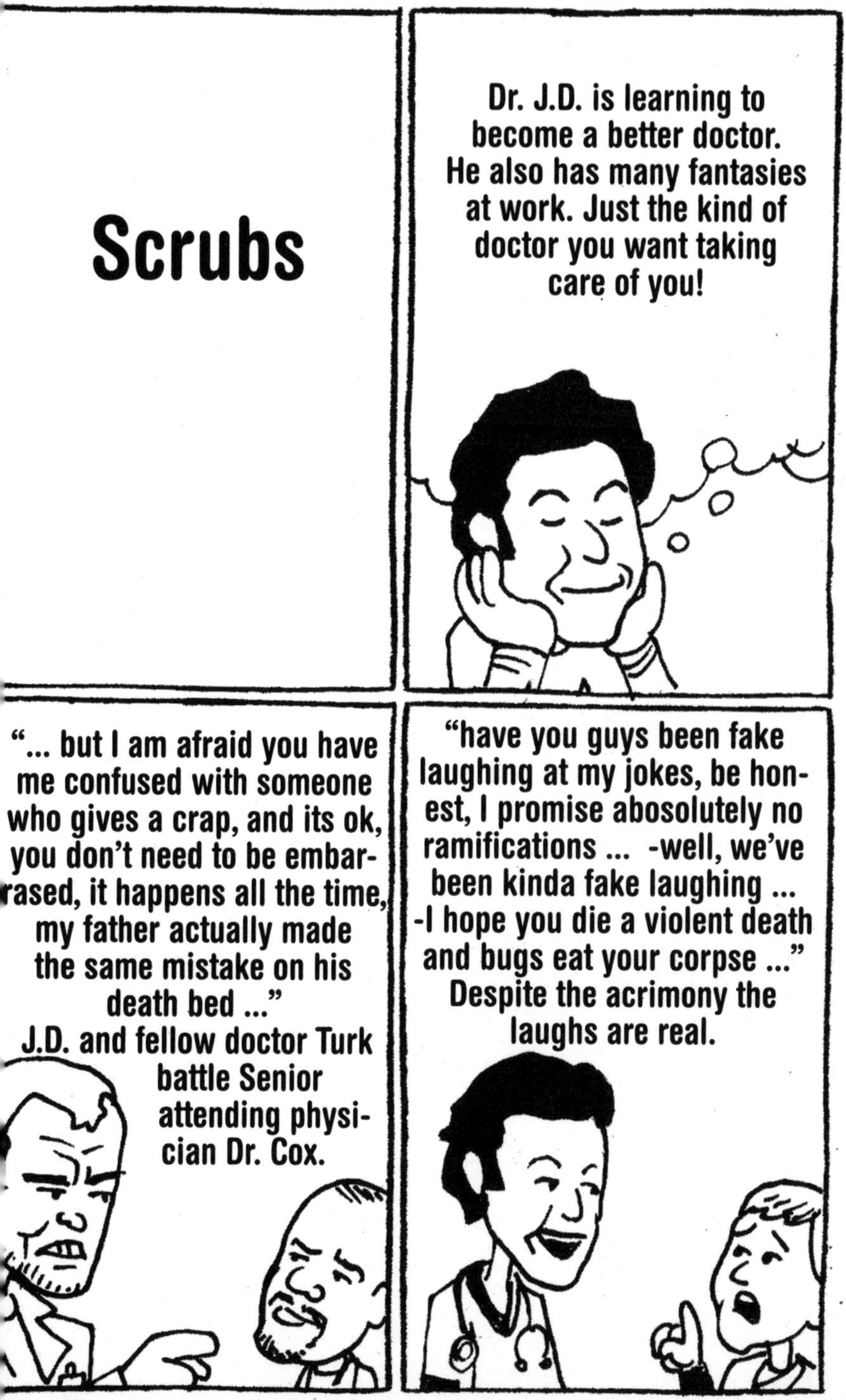
Scrubs
Dr. J.D. is learning to become a better doctor. He also has many fantasies at work. Just the kind of doctor you want taking care of you!
"... but I am afraid you have me confused with someone who gives a crap, and its ok, you don't need to be embar-rased, it happens all the time, my father actually made the same mistake on his death bed ..."
J.D. and fellow doctor Turk battle Senior attending physi-cian Dr. Cox.
"have you guys been fake laughing at my jokes, be hon-est, I promise abosolutely no ramifications ... -well, we've been kinda fake laughing ... -I hope you die a violent death and bugs eat your corpse ..."
Despite the acrimony the laughs are real.

South Park

"Oh my god. Jay Leno's chin killed Kenny. You bastard."

Stan, Kyle, Kenny, and Cartman, and Kenny are best friends. Kenny dies every episode.

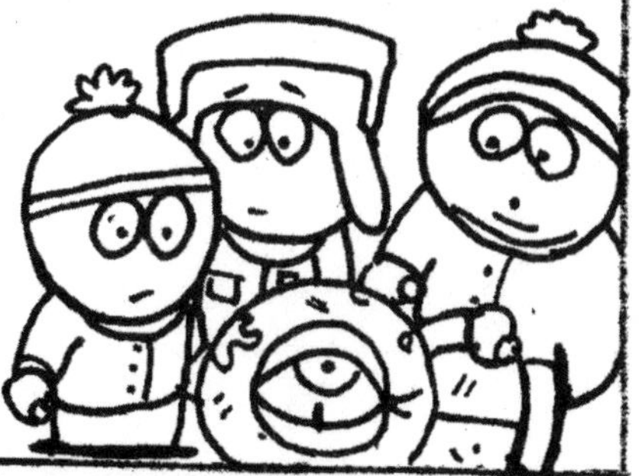

"Come on, children. Let's go find ourselves a nice white woman to make love to."

The school cafeteria is run by Chef.

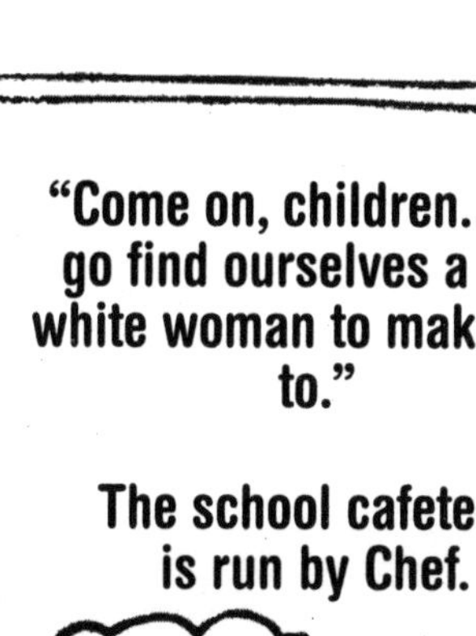
CHEF

"The rest of you go get the goods on Stan. His mom grounded him once for setting something on fire. Let's find out what that something was and then lie and say it was a puppy."
Cartman always tries to get the upper hand.

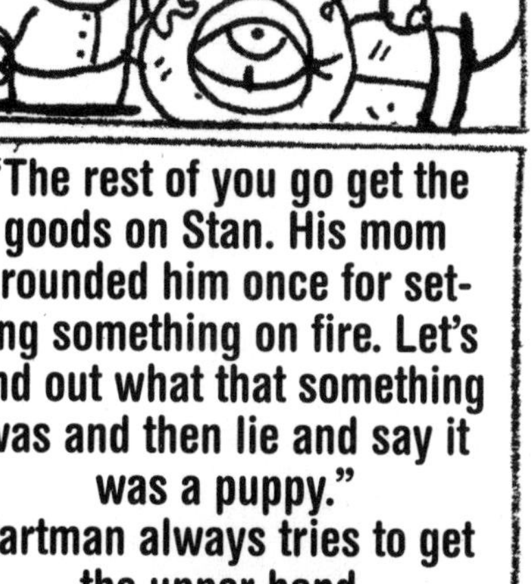

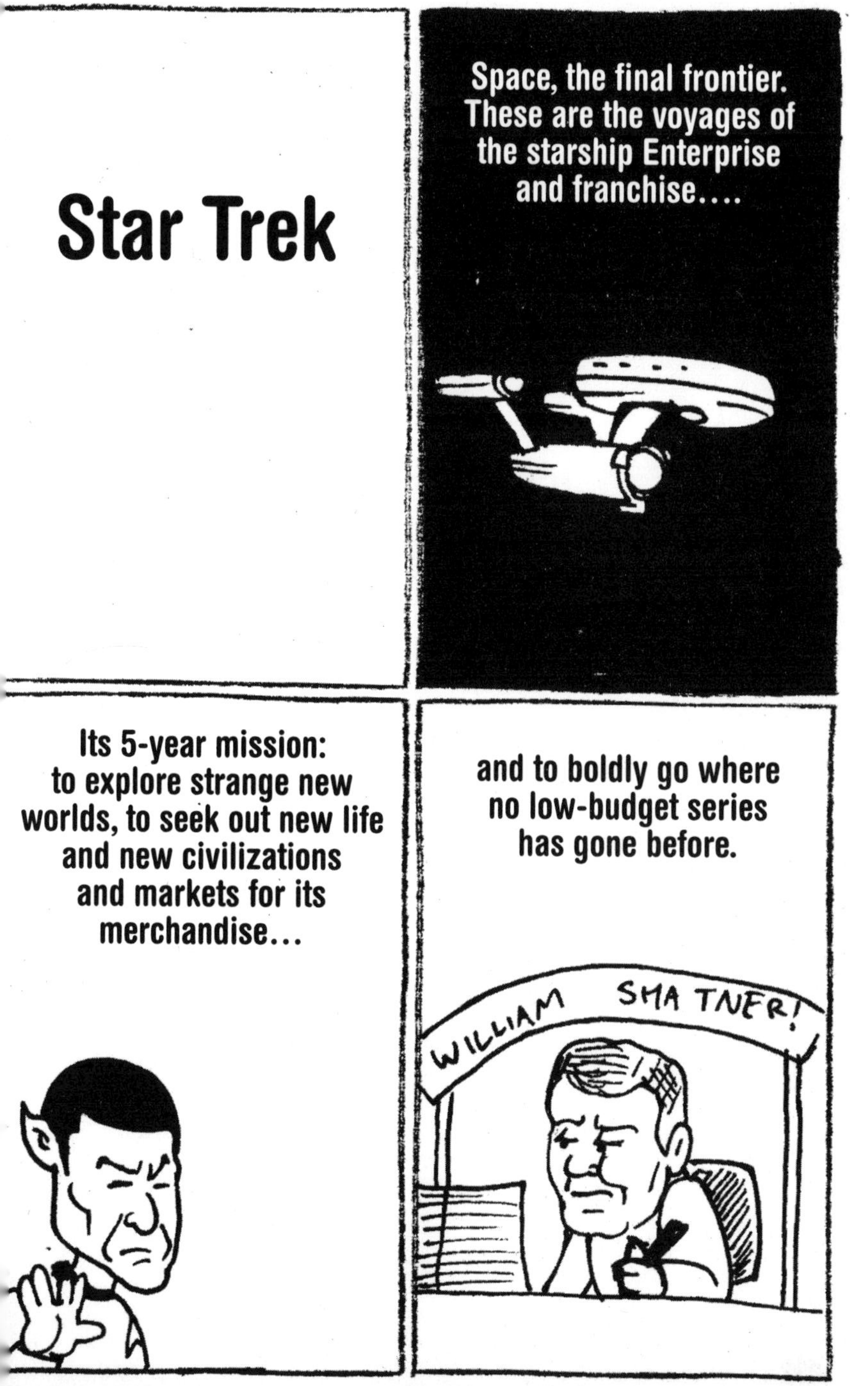
Star Trek
Space, the final frontier.
These are the voyages of
the starship Enterprise
and franchise....
Its 5-year mission:
to explore strange new
worlds, to seek out new life
and new civilizations
and markets for its
merchandise...
and to boldly go where
no low-budget series
has gone before.
WILLIAM SHATNER!

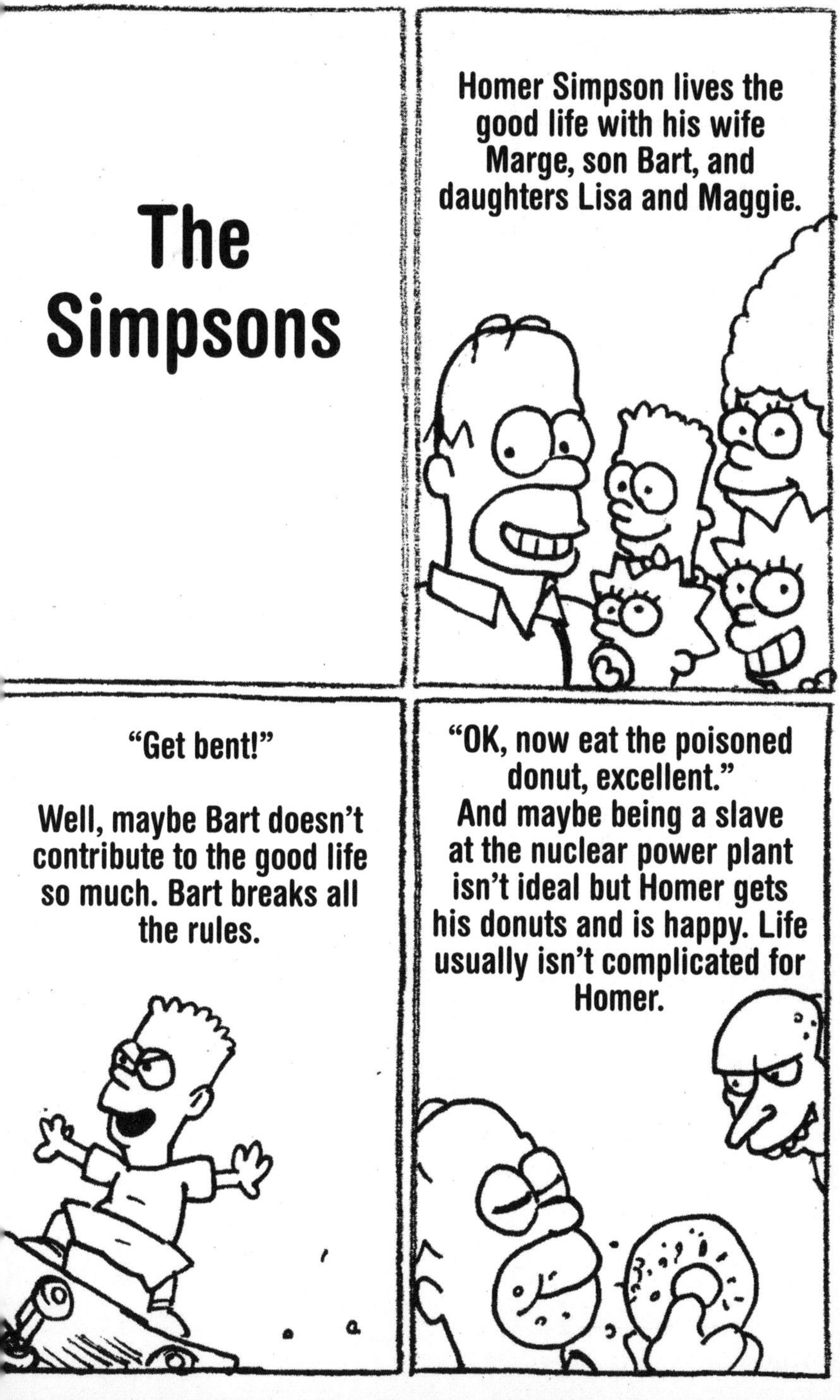
The Simpsons
Homer Simpson lives the good life with his wife Marge, son Bart, and daughters Lisa and Maggie.
"Get bent!"
Well, maybe Bart doesn't contribute to the good life so much. Bart breaks all the rules.
"OK, now eat the poisoned donut, excellent."
And maybe being a slave at the nuclear power plant isn't ideal but Homer gets his donuts and is happy. Life usually isn't complicated for Homer.

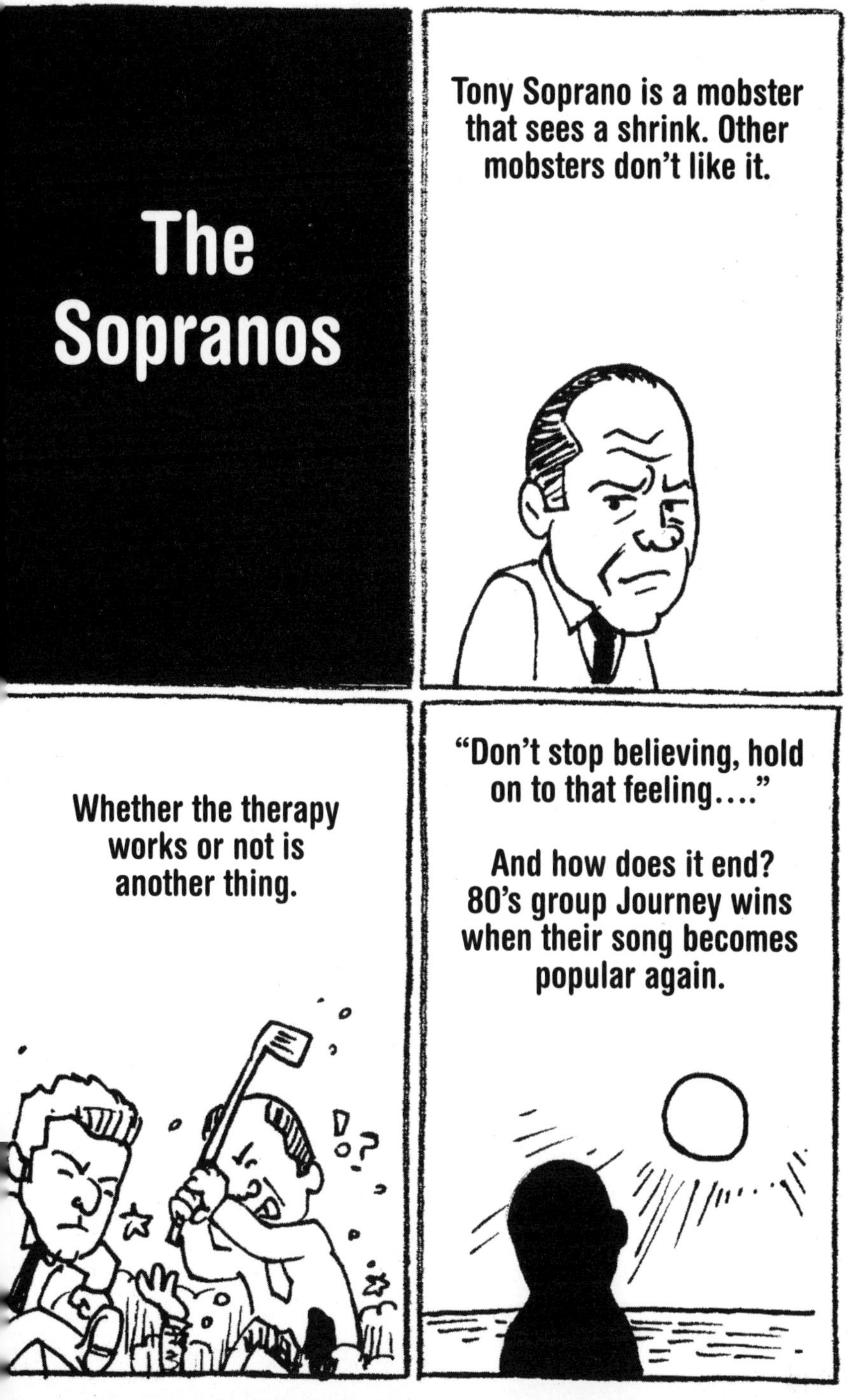
The Sopranos
Tony Soprano is a mobster that sees a shrink. Other mobsters don't like it.
Whether the therapy works or not is another thing.
"Don't stop believing, hold on to that feeling...."
And how does it end? 80's group Journey wins when their song becomes popular again.

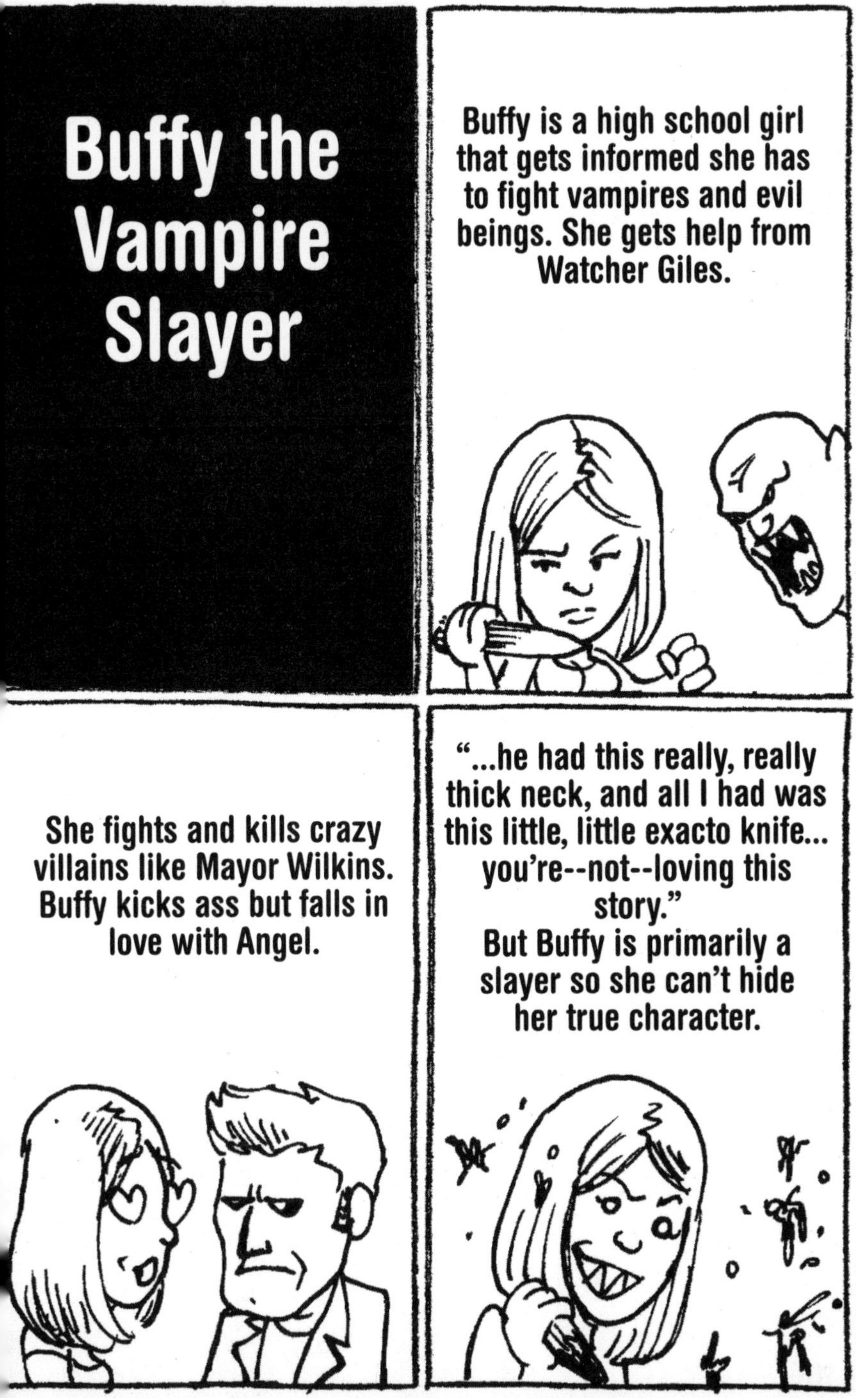
Buffy the Vampire Slayer
Buffy is a high school girl that gets informed she has to fight vampires and evil beings. She gets help from Watcher Giles.
She fights and kills crazy villains like Mayor Wilkins. Buffy kicks ass but falls in love with Angel.
"...he had this really, really thick neck, and all I had was this little, little exacto knife... you're--not--loving this story."
But Buffy is primarily a slayer so she can't hide her true character.

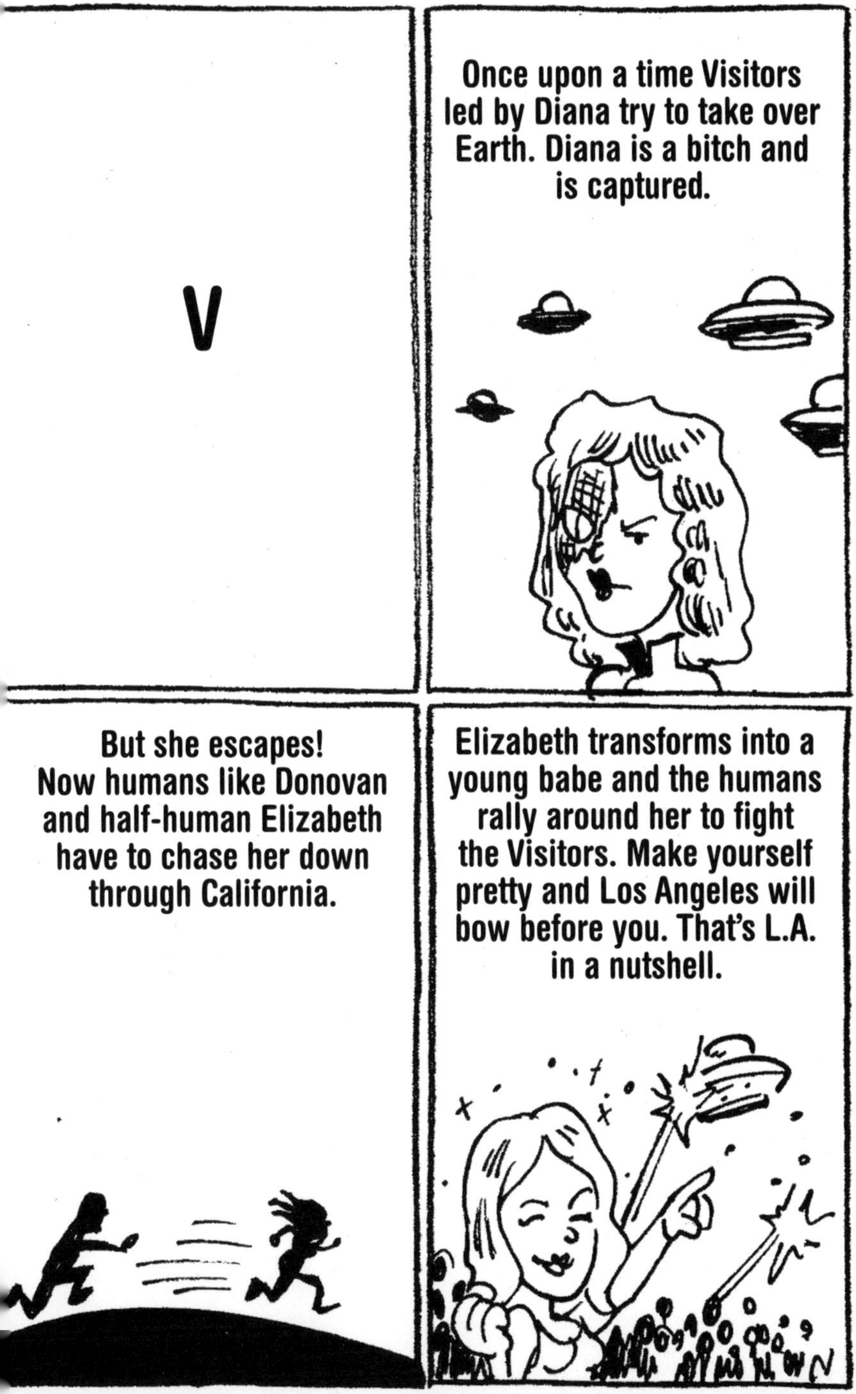
V
Once upon a time Visitors led by Diana try to take over Earth. Diana is a bitch and is captured.
But she escapes! Now humans like Donovan and half-human Elizabeth have to chase her down through California.
Elizabeth transforms into a young babe and the humans rally around her to fight the Visitors. Make yourself pretty and Los Angeles will bow before you. That's L.A. in a nutshell.

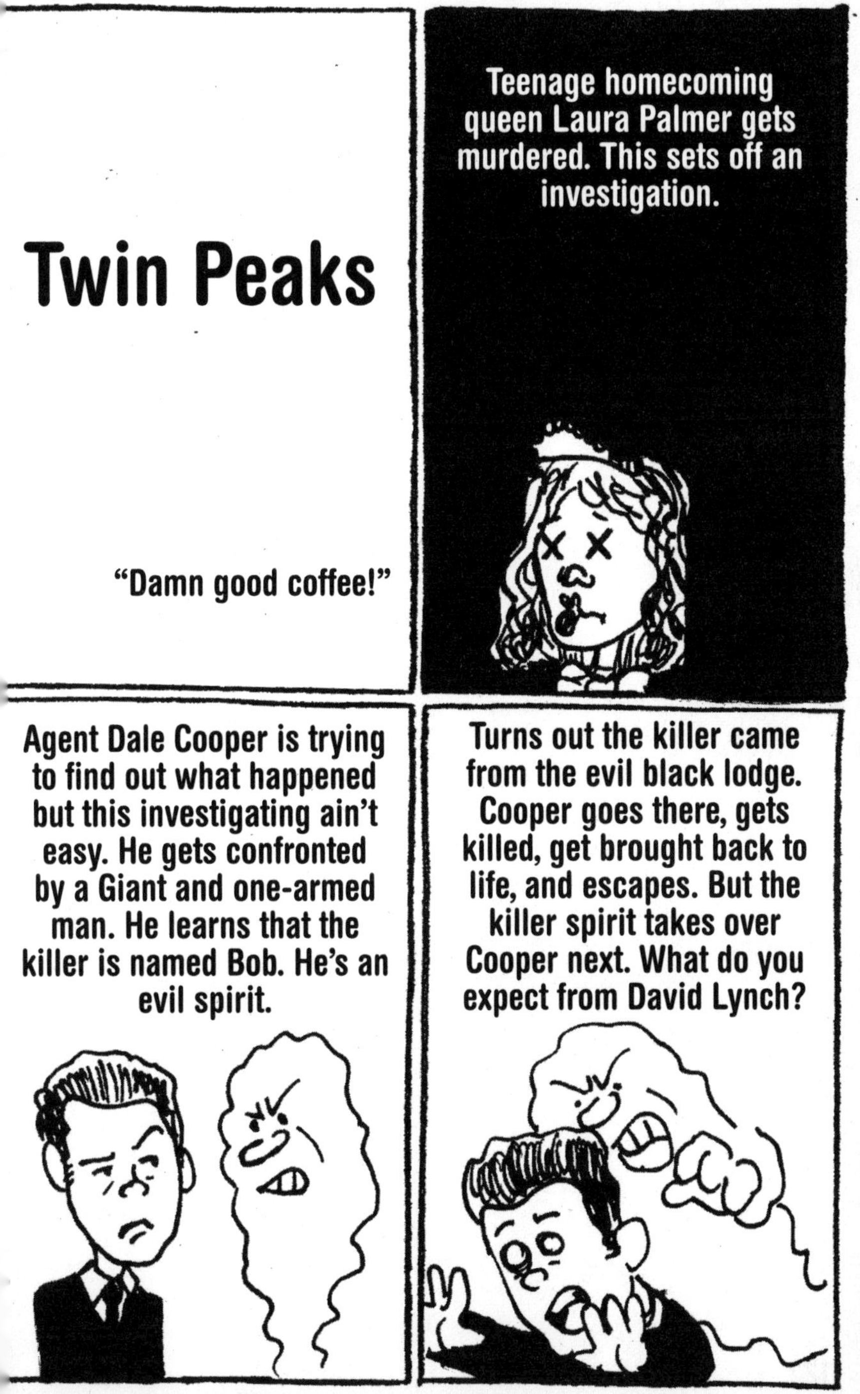
Twin Peaks
"Damn good coffee!"
Teenage homecoming queen Laura Palmer gets murdered. This sets off an investigation.
Agent Dale Cooper is trying to find out what happened but this investigating ain't easy. He gets confronted by a Giant and one-armed man. He learns that the killer is named Bob. He's an evil spirit.
Turns out the killer came from the evil black lodge. Cooper goes there, gets killed, get brought back to life, and escapes. But the killer spirit takes over Cooper next. What do you expect from David Lynch?

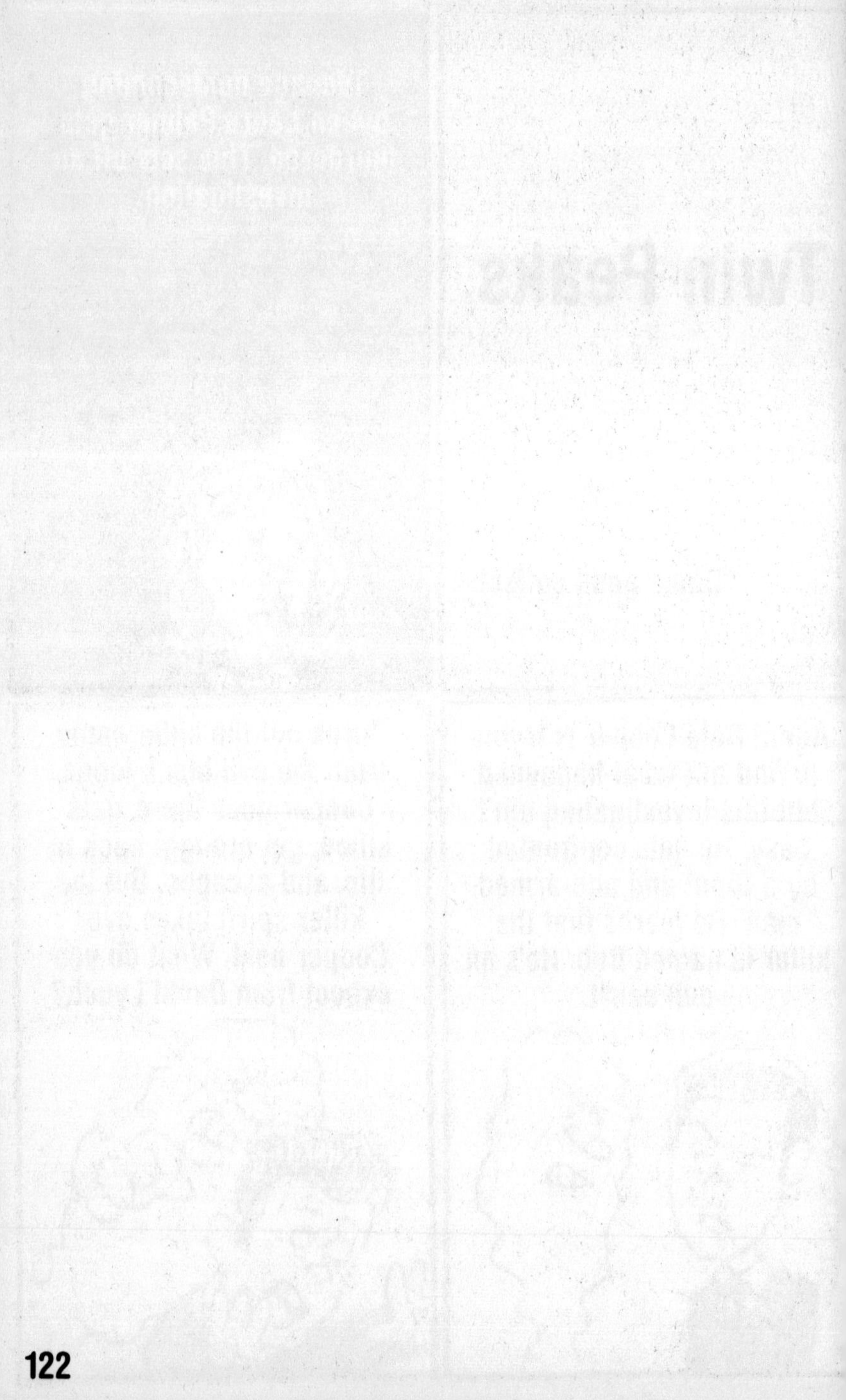
Twin Peaks

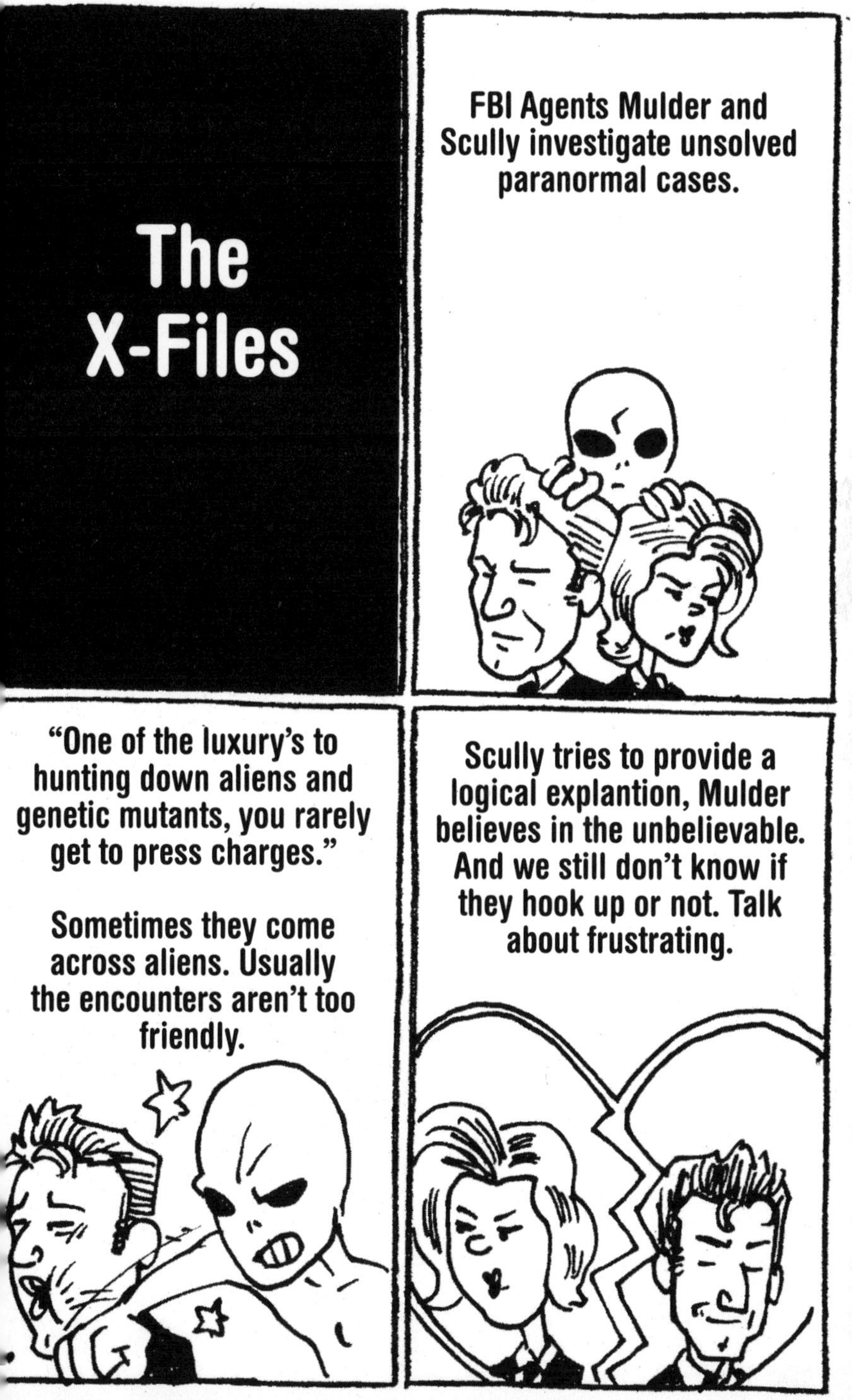
The X-Files
FBI Agents Mulder and Scully investigate unsolved paranormal cases.
"One of the luxury's to hunting down aliens and genetic mutants, you rarely get to press charges."
Sometimes they come across aliens. Usually the encounters aren't too friendly.
Scully tries to provide a logical explantion, Mulder believes in the unbelievable. And we still don't know if they hook up or not. Talk about frustrating.

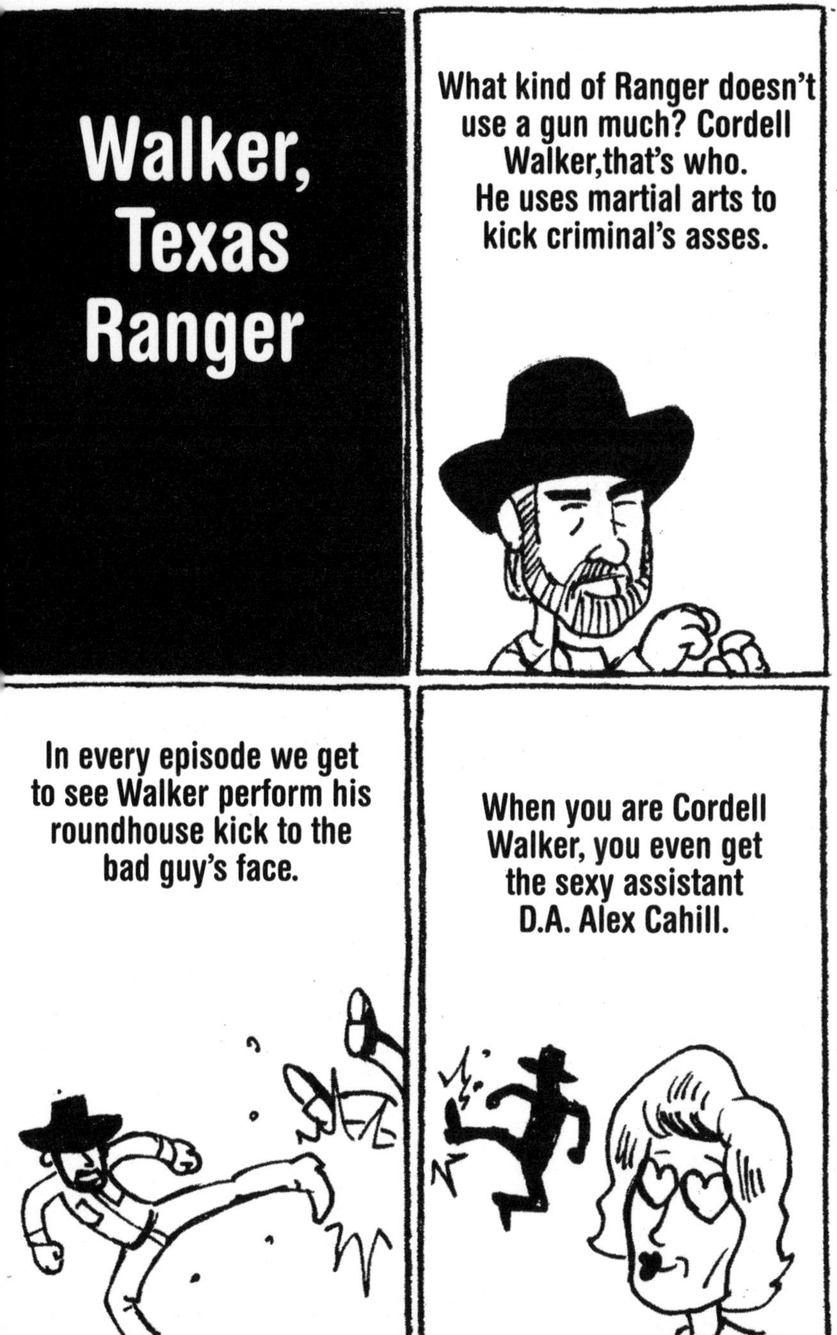
Walker, Texas Ranger
What kind of Ranger doesn't use a gun much? Cordell Walker,that's who. He uses martial arts to kick criminal's asses.
In every episode we get to see Walker perform his roundhouse kick to the bad guy's face.
When you are Cordell Walker, you even get the sexy assistant D.A. Alex Cahill.

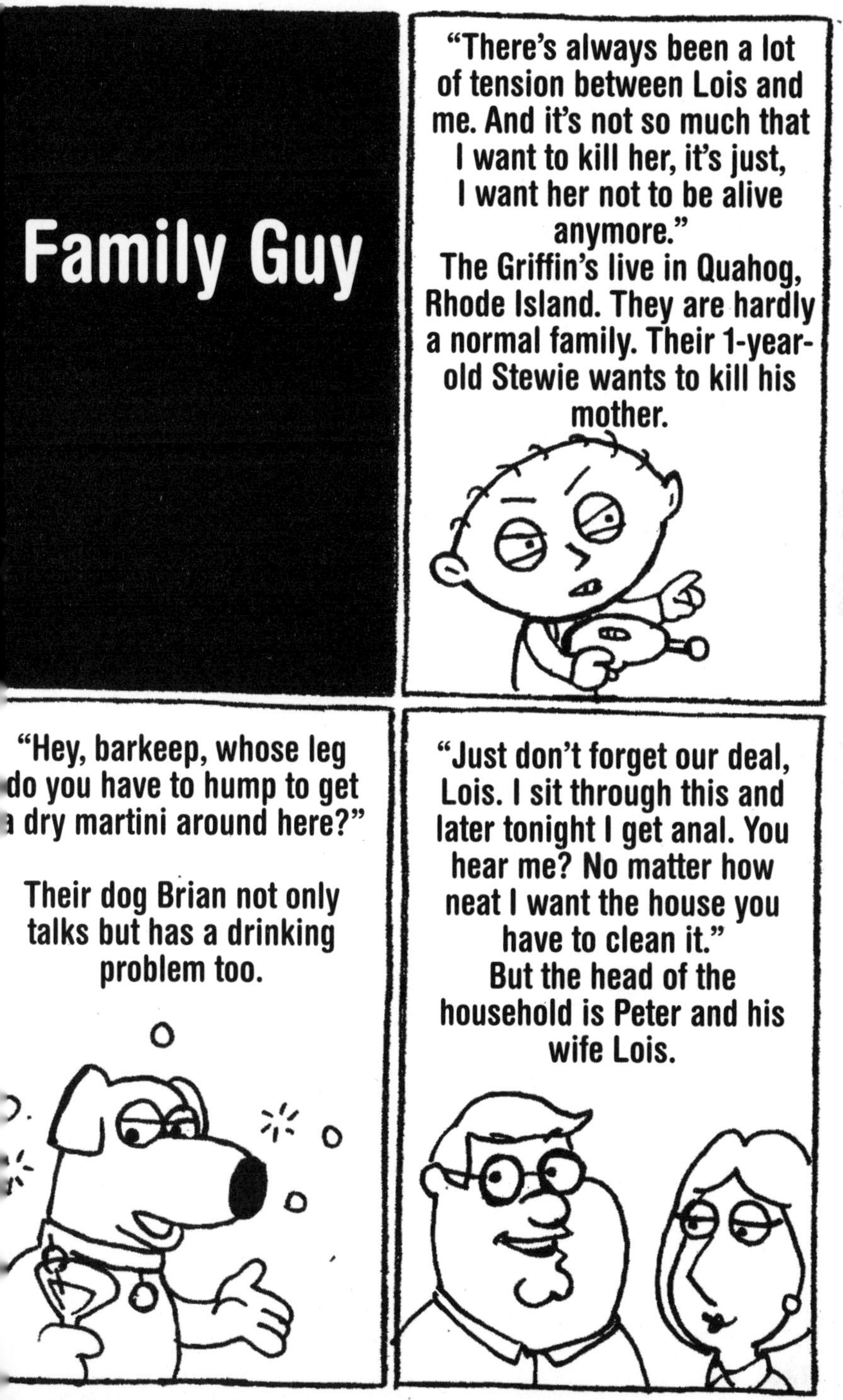

Family Guy
"There's always been a lot of tension between Lois and me. And it's not so much that I want to kill her, it's just, I want her not to be alive anymore."
The Griffin's live in Quahog, Rhode Island. They are hardly a normal family. Their 1-year-old Stewie wants to kill his mother.
"Hey, barkeep, whose leg do you have to hump to get a dry martini around here?"
Their dog Brian not only talks but has a drinking problem too.
"Just don't forget our deal, Lois. I sit through this and later tonight I get anal. You hear me? No matter how neat I want the house you have to clean it."
But the head of the household is Peter and his wife Lois.

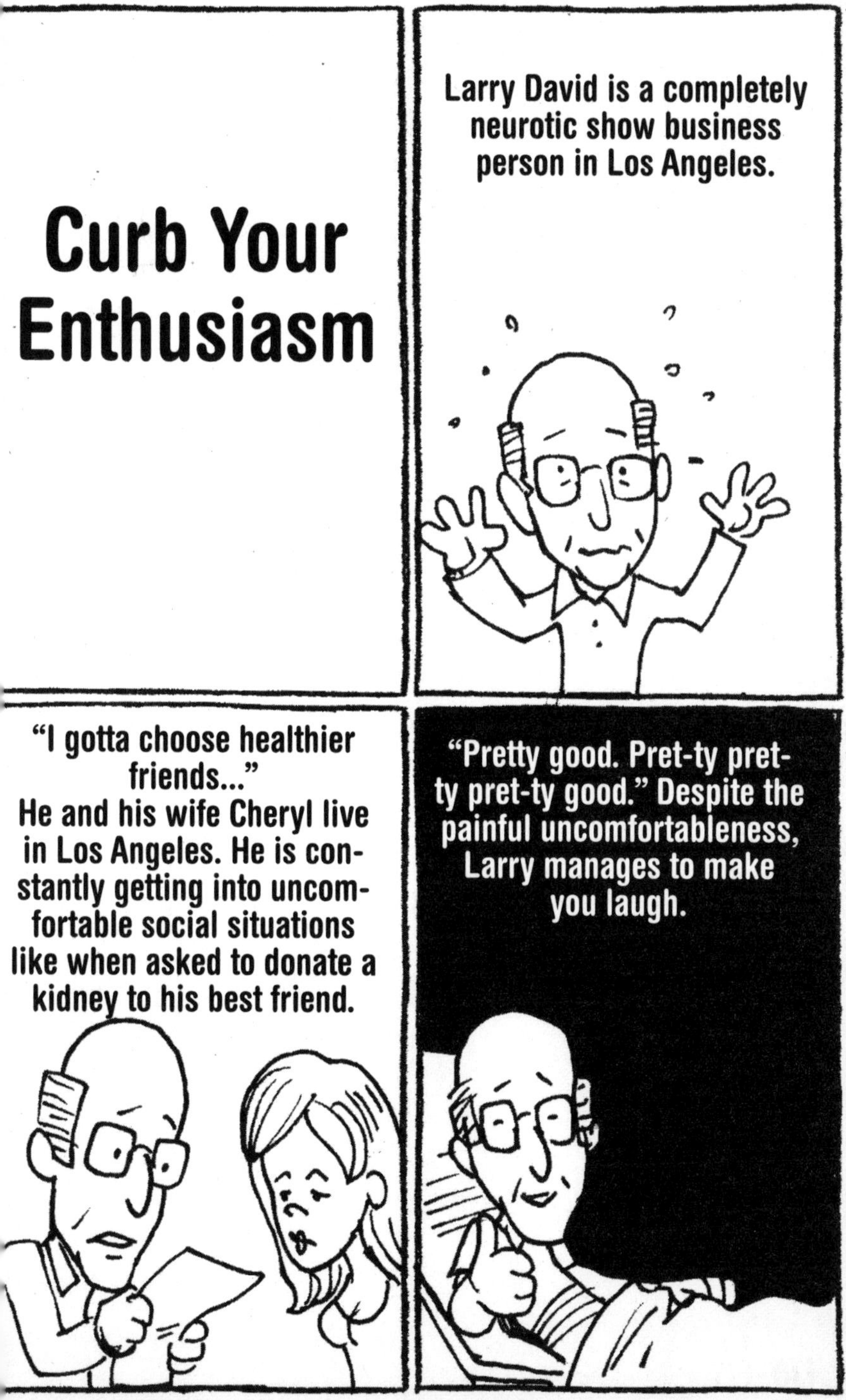
Curb Your Enthusiasm
Larry David is a completely neurotic show business person in Los Angeles.
"I gotta choose healthier friends..." He and his wife Cheryl live in Los Angeles. He is constantly getting into uncomfortable social situations like when asked to donate a kidney to his best friend.
"Pretty good. Pret-ty pretty pret-ty good." Despite the painful uncomfortableness, Larry manages to make you laugh.

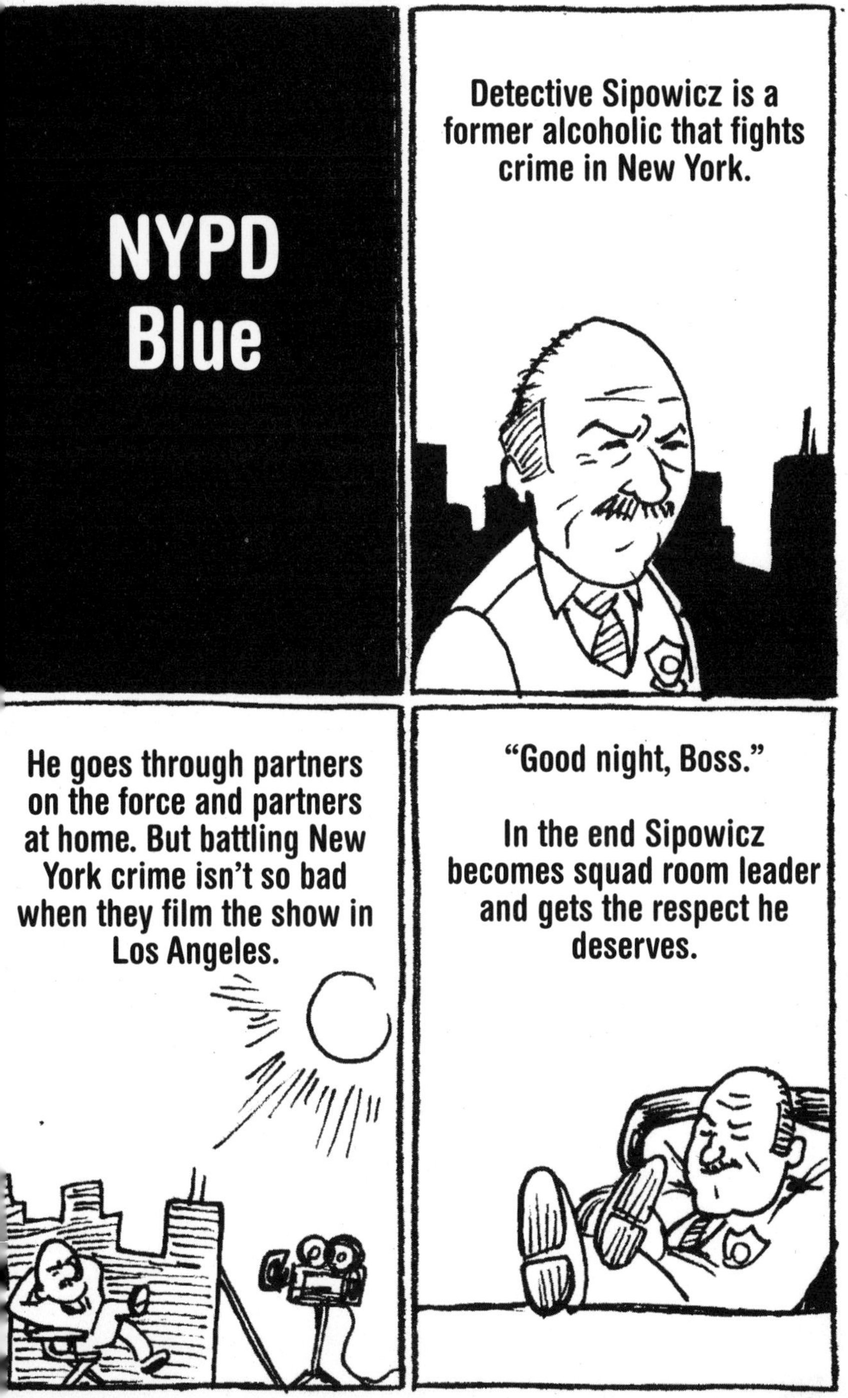
NYPD Blue
Detective Sipowicz is a former alcoholic that fights crime in New York.
He goes through partners on the force and partners at home. But battling New York crime isn't so bad when they film the show in Los Angeles.
"Good night, Boss."
In the end Sipowicz becomes squad room leader and gets the respect he deserves.

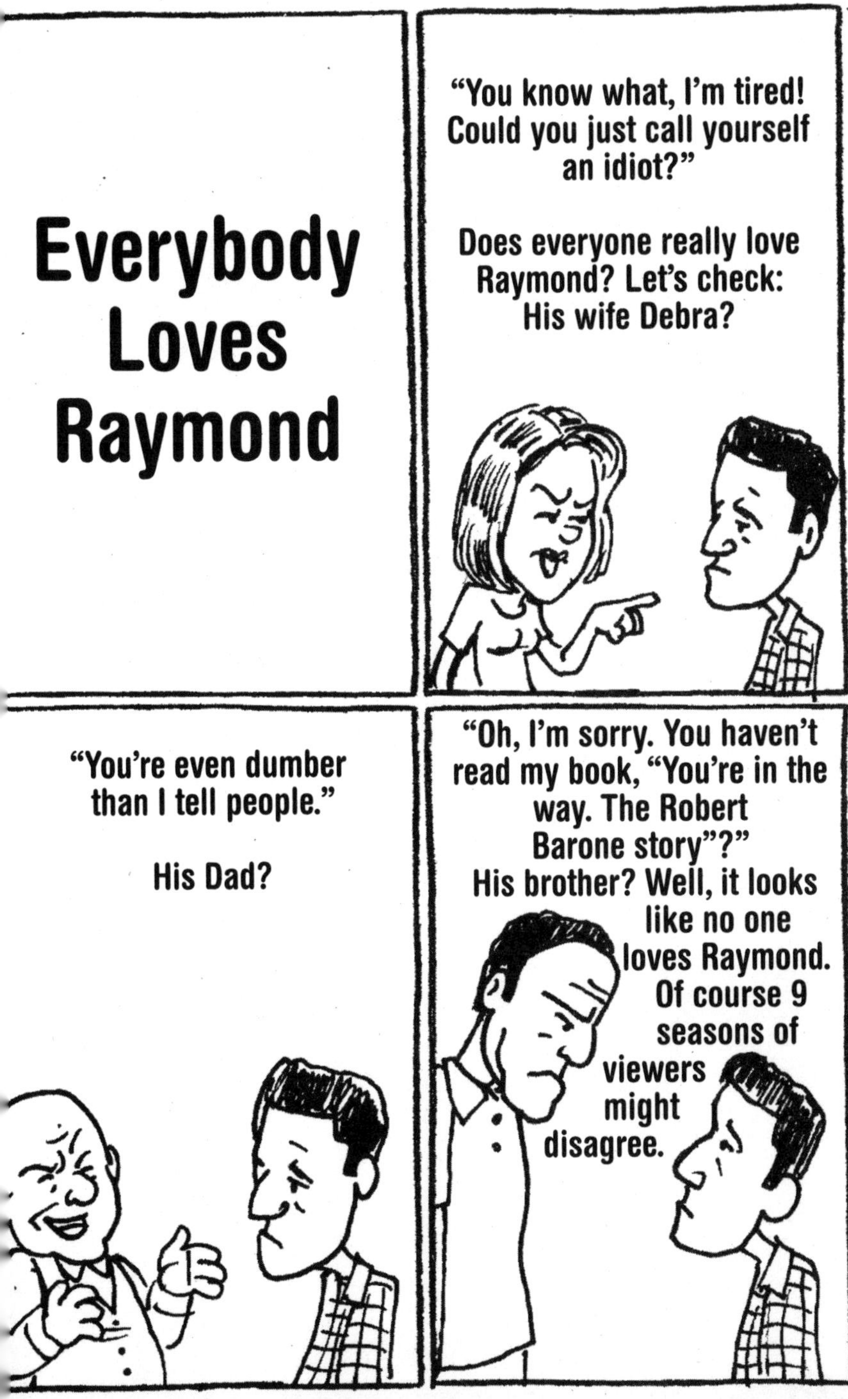
Everybody Loves Raymond
"You know what, I'm tired! Could you just call yourself an idiot?"
Does everyone really love Raymond? Let's check: His wife Debra?
"You're even dumber than I tell people."
His Dad?
"Oh, I'm sorry. You haven't read my book, "You're in the way. The Robert Barone story"?"
His brother? Well, it looks like no one loves Raymond. Of course 9 seasons of viewers might disagree.

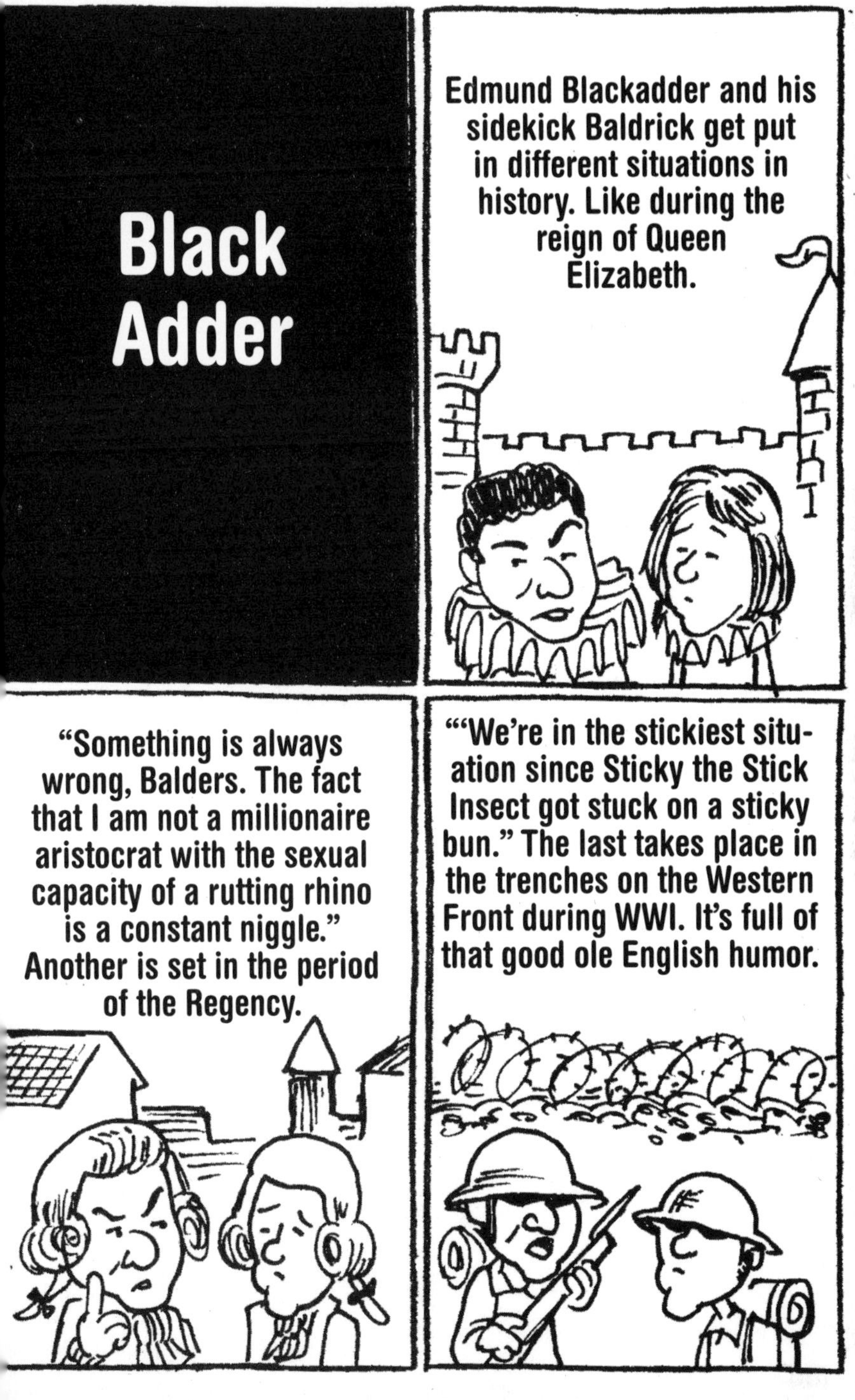
Black Adder
Edmund Blackadder and his sidekick Baldrick get put in different situations in history. Like during the reign of Queen Elizabeth.
"Something is always wrong, Balders. The fact that I am not a millionaire aristocrat with the sexual capacity of a rutting rhino is a constant niggle." Another is set in the period of the Regency.
""We're in the stickiest situation since Sticky the Stick Insect got stuck on a sticky bun." The last takes place in the trenches on the Western Front during WWI. It's full of that good ole English humor.

King of the Hill

"You can give me the stink eye all you want, but it's not gonna change anything."
White trash cartoon fun with Hank Hill!

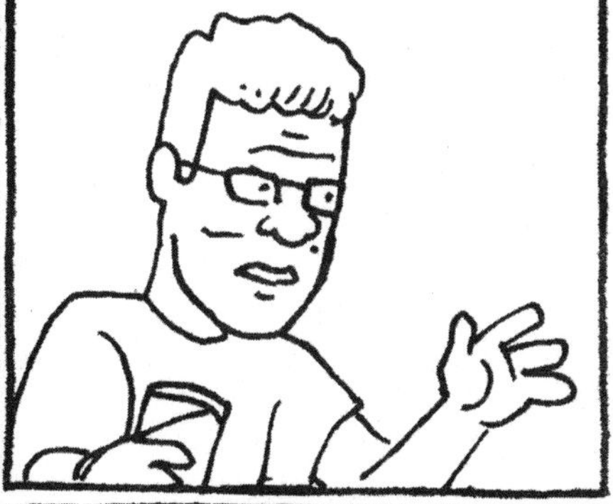

"All right! I'm in a team with my dad. Permision to lead the team in a cheer. Give me a..."
"Permision denied."
Hank does stuff like bond with his son Bobby.

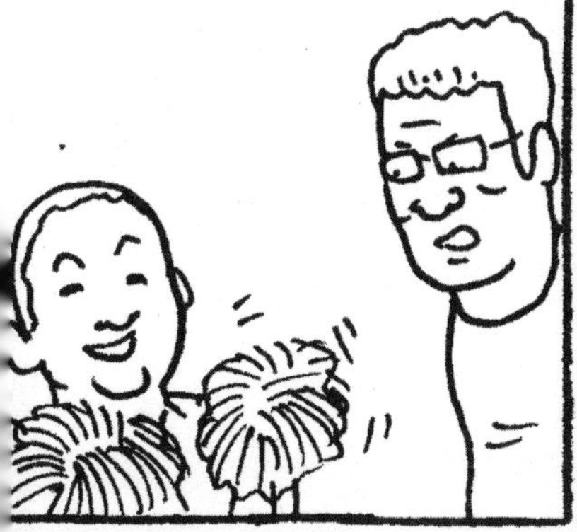

"Earth first.
Make Mars our bitch."
Anything goes when you are white trash living in Texas. Even if you are trying to be environmentally sensitive.

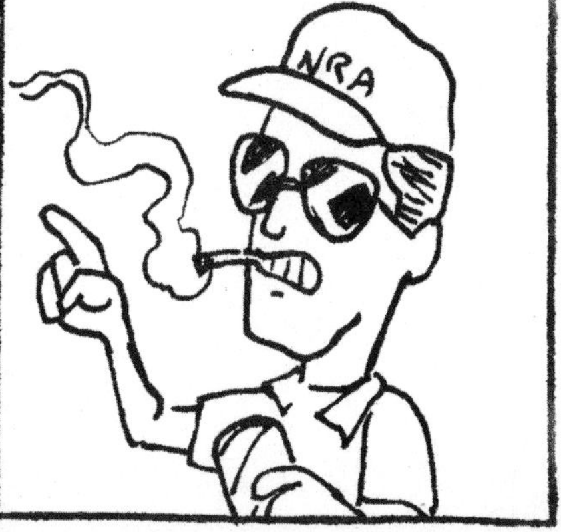
NRA

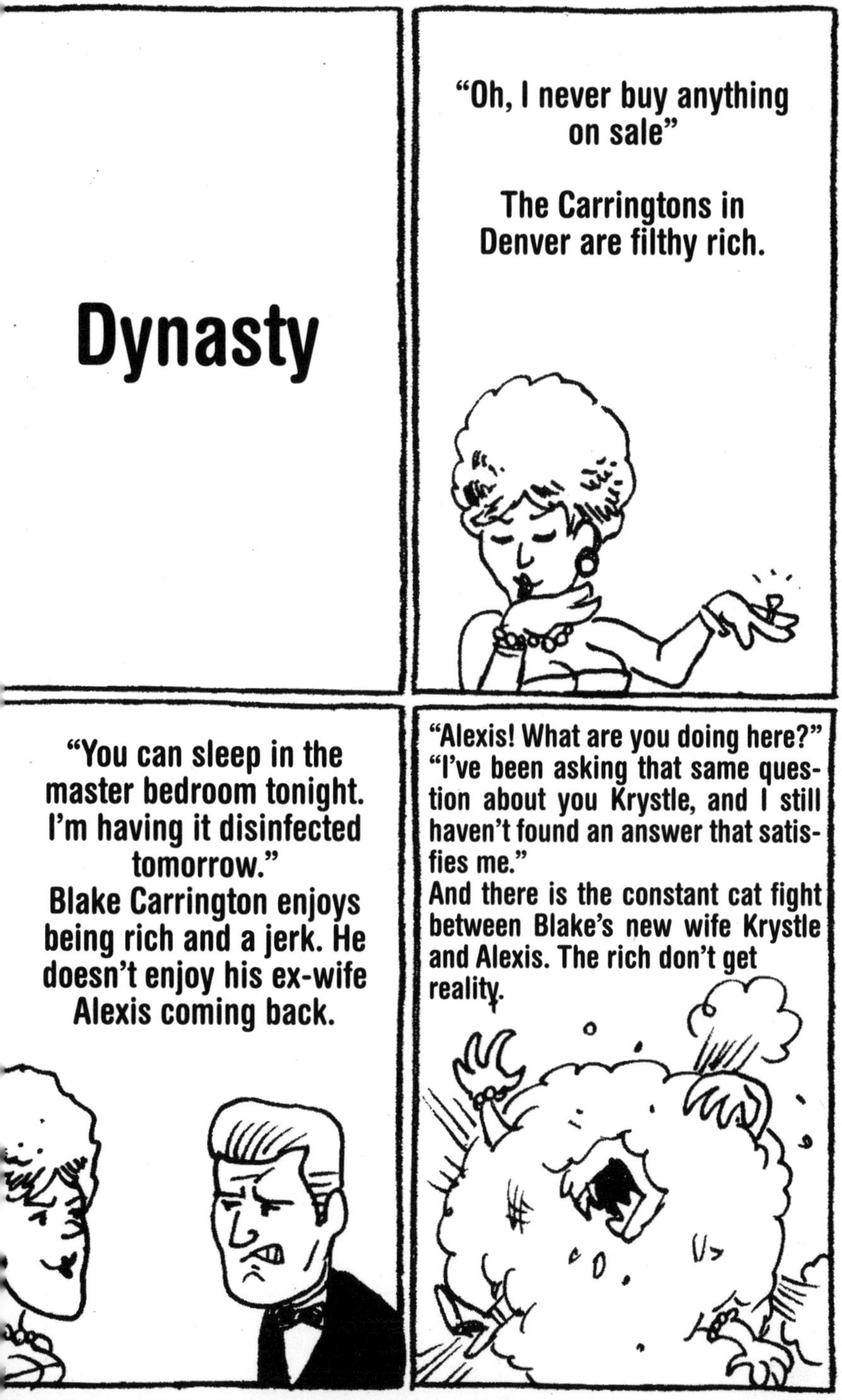
Dynasty
“Oh, I never buy anything on sale”
The Carringtons in Denver are filthy rich.
“You can sleep in the master bedroom tonight. I’m having it disinfected tomorrow.”
Blake Carrington enjoys being rich and a jerk. He doesn’t enjoy his ex-wife Alexis coming back.
“Alexis! What are you doing here?”
“I’ve been asking that same question about you Krystle, and I still haven’t found an answer that satisfies me.”
And there is the constant cat fight between Blake’s new wife Krystle and Alexis. The rich don’t get reality.

Little House on the Prarie

Charles Ingalls is stuck on a farm in Minnesota in the 1880's. His daughters Mary, Laura, Caroline, and Grace wish TV was invented and pretend to like nature.

Albert gets adopted into this family of 4 daughters. Guess who is groomed to take out the trash? The only son. Lucky Albert.

"Your ma's right, half-pint. Now on the way home, I'll teach you about blackmail and extortion for your friend Nellie." Laura is constantly battling Nellie Oleson. But Charles is very wise and teaches Laura that kicking Nellie's ass might not be the proper thing on the prarie.

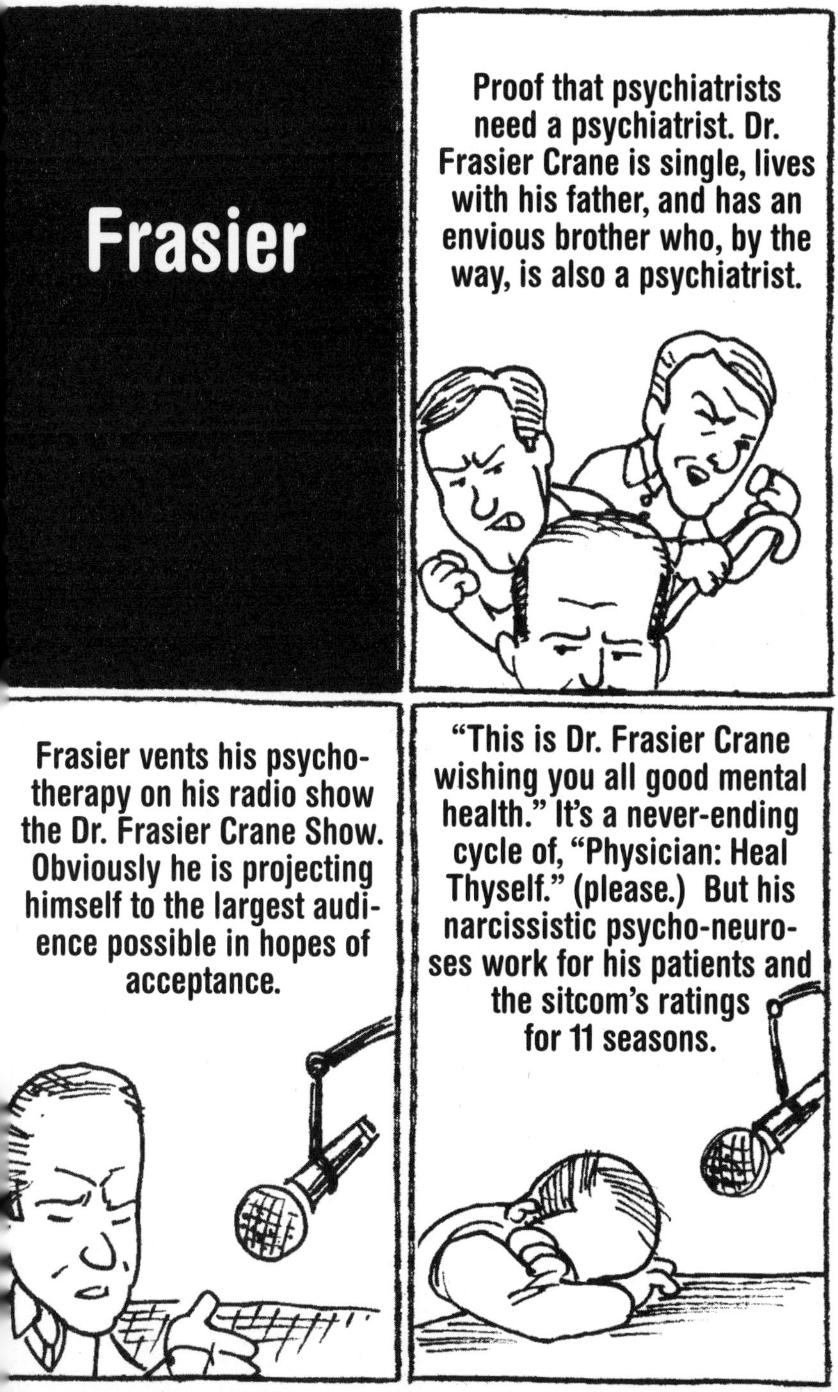
Frasier
Proof that psychiatrists need a psychiatrist. Dr. Frasier Crane is single, lives with his father, and has an envious brother who, by the way, is also a psychiatrist.
Frasier vents his psychotherapy on his radio show the Dr. Frasier Crane Show. Obviously he is projecting himself to the largest audience possible in hopes of acceptance.
"This is Dr. Frasier Crane wishing you all good mental health." It's a never-ending cycle of, "Physician: Heal Thyself." (please.) But his narcissistic psycho-neuroses work for his patients and the sitcom's ratings for 11 seasons.

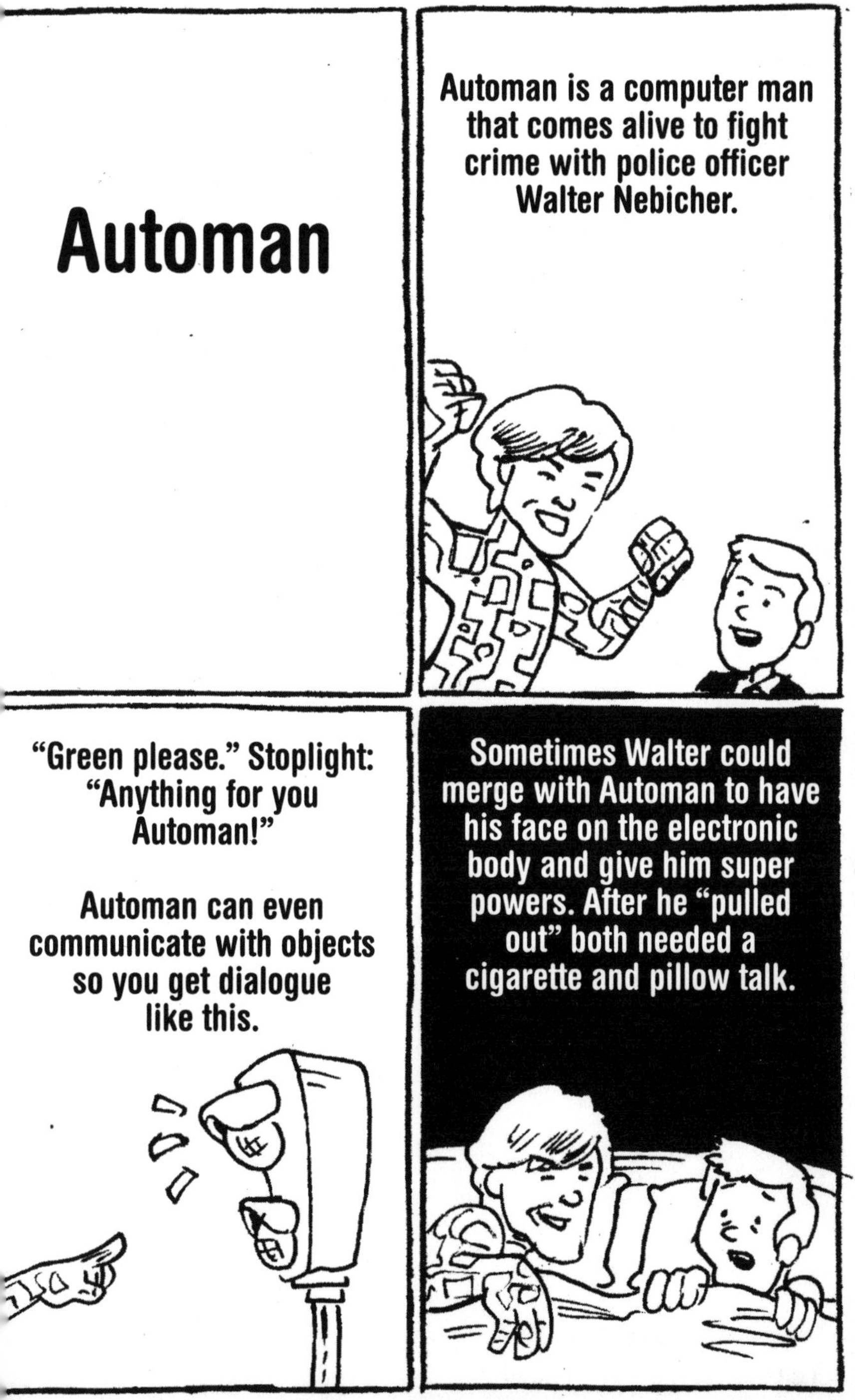
Automan
Automan is a computer man that comes alive to fight crime with police officer Walter Nebicher.
"Green please." Stoplight: "Anything for you Automan!"
Automan can even communicate with objects so you get dialogue like this.
Sometimes Walter could merge with Automan to have his face on the electronic body and give him super powers. After he "pulled out" both needed a cigarette and pillow talk.

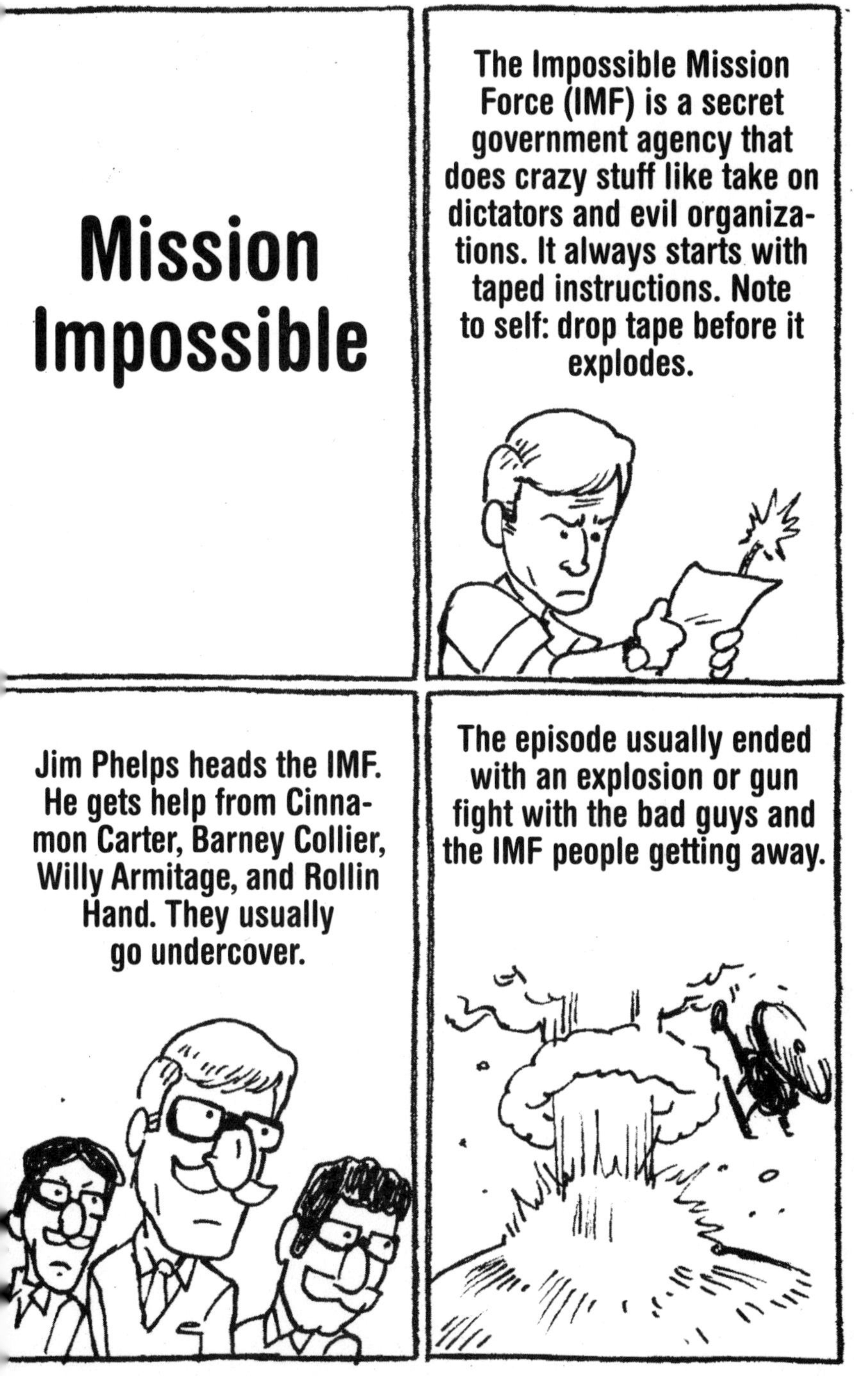
Mission Impossible
The Impossible Mission Force (IMF) is a secret government agency that does crazy stuff like take on dictators and evil organizations. It always starts with taped instructions. Note to self: drop tape before it explodes.
Jim Phelps heads the IMF. He gets help from Cinnamon Carter, Barney Collier, Willy Armitage, and Rollin Hand. They usually go undercover.
The episode usually ended with an explosion or gun fight with the bad guys and the IMF people getting away.

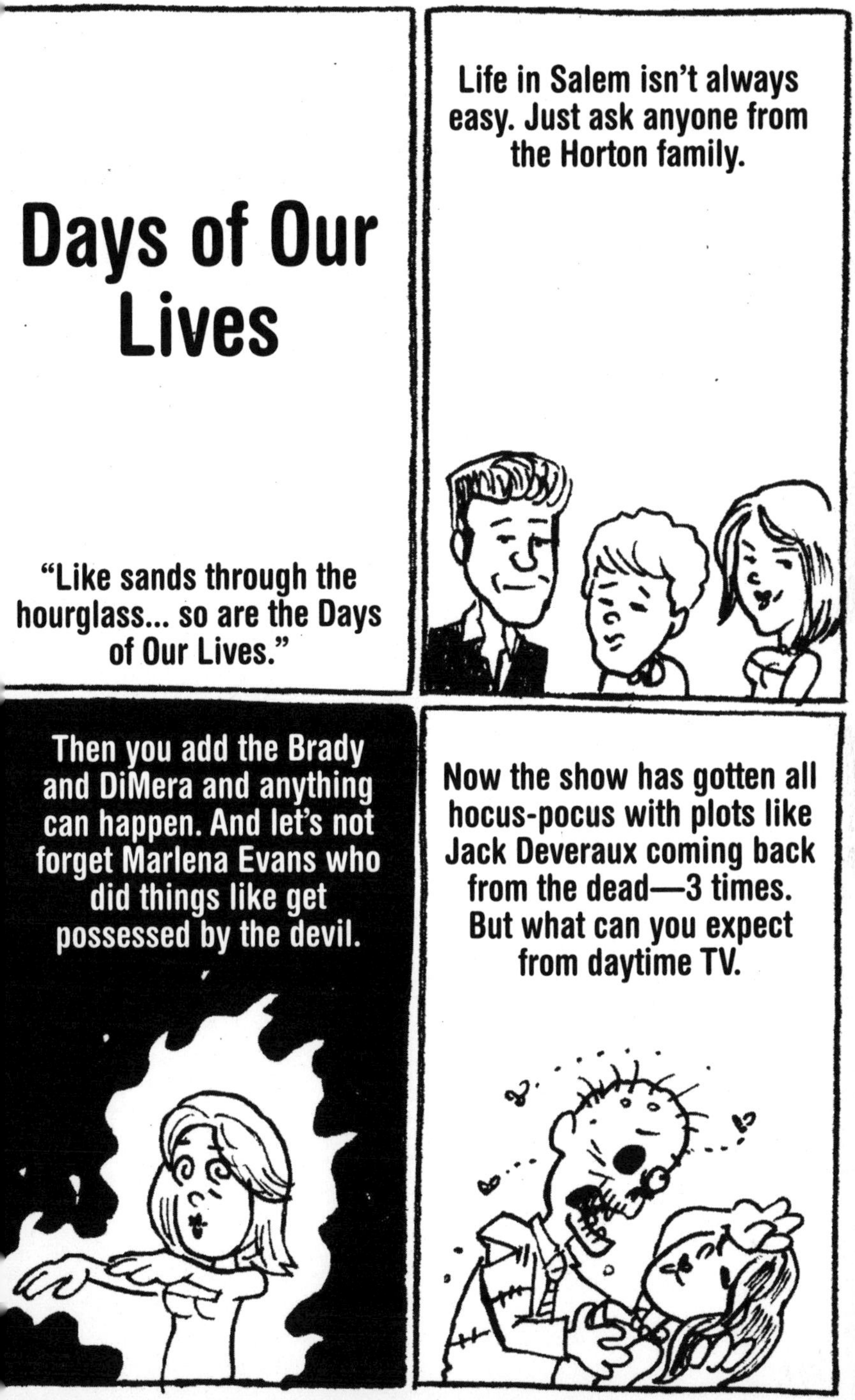
Days of Our Lives
"Like sands through the hourglass... so are the Days of Our Lives."
Life in Salem isn't always easy. Just ask anyone from the Horton family.
Then you add the Brady and DiMera and anything can happen. And let's not forget Marlena Evans who did things like get possessed by the devil.
Now the show has gotten all hocus-pocus with plots like Jack Deveraux coming back from the dead—3 times. But what can you expect from daytime TV.

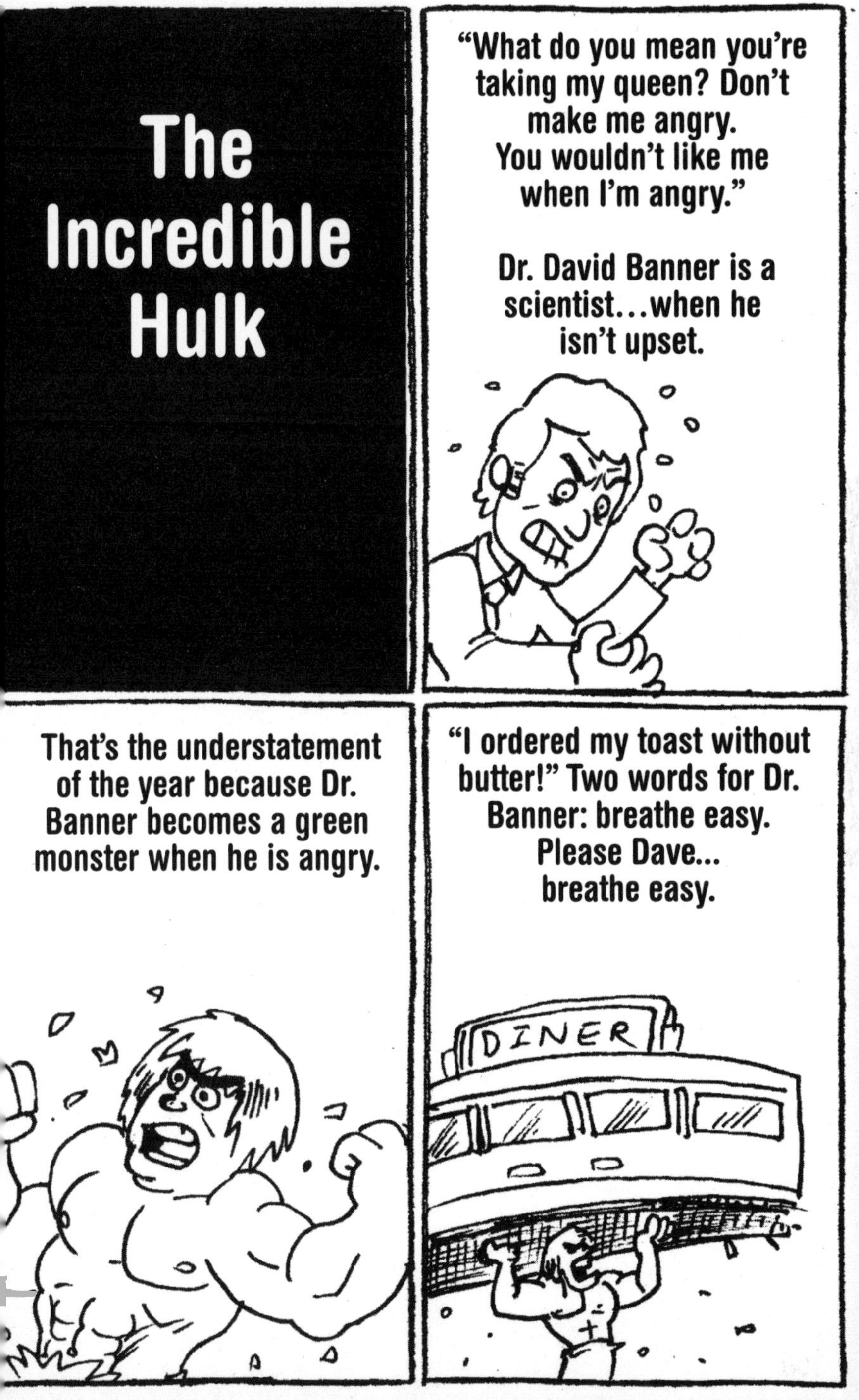
The Incredible Hulk
"What do you mean you're taking my queen? Don't make me angry. You wouldn't like me when I'm angry."
Dr. David Banner is a scientist…when he isn't upset.
That's the understatement of the year because Dr. Banner becomes a green monster when he is angry.
"I ordered my toast without butter!" Two words for Dr. Banner: breathe easy. Please Dave... breathe easy.
DINER

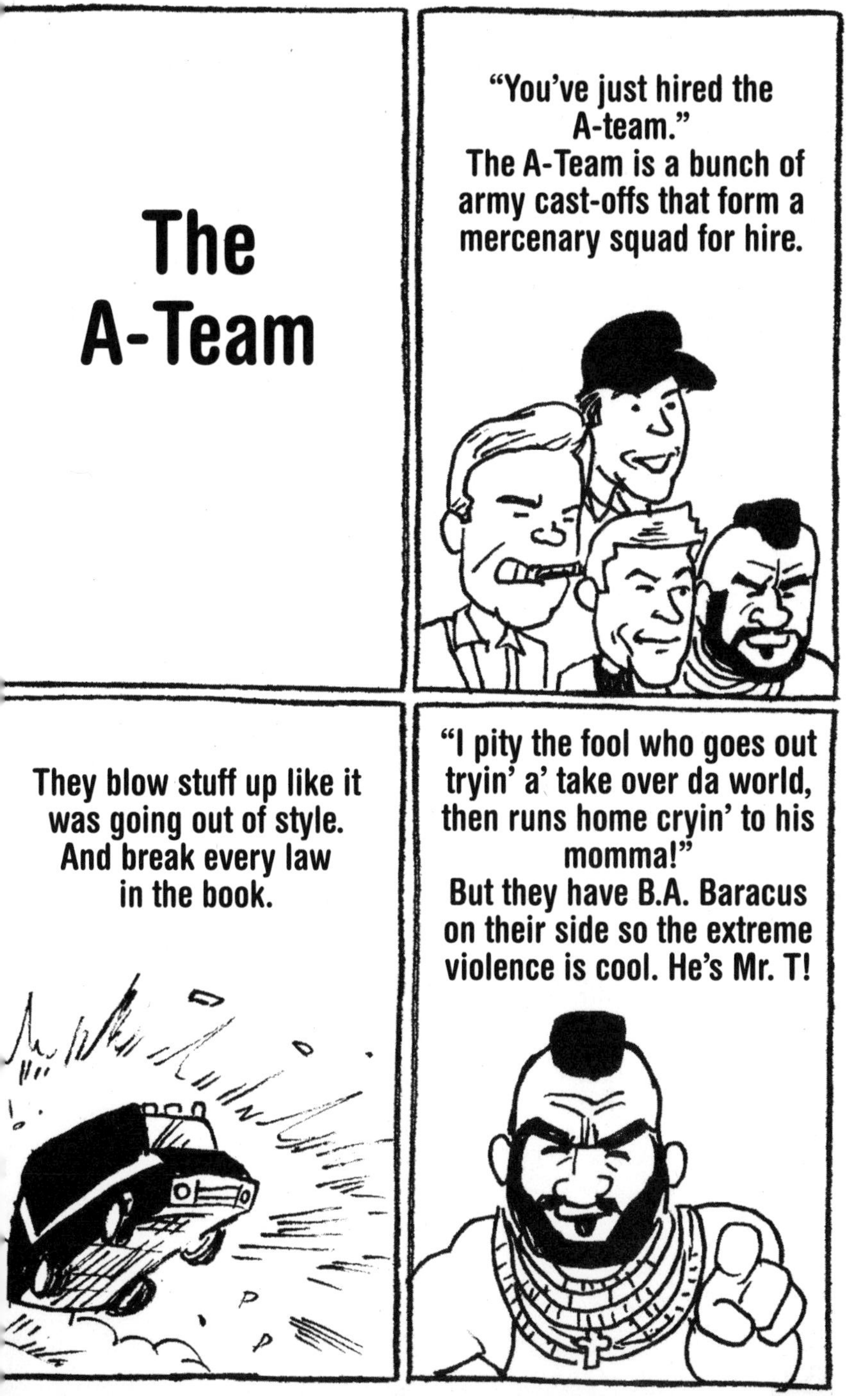
The A-Team
"You've just hired the A-team."
The A-Team is a bunch of army cast-offs that form a mercenary squad for hire.
They blow stuff up like it was going out of style. And break every law in the book.
"I pity the fool who goes out tryin' a' take over da world, then runs home cryin' to his momma!"
But they have B.A. Baracus on their side so the extreme violence is cool. He's Mr. T!

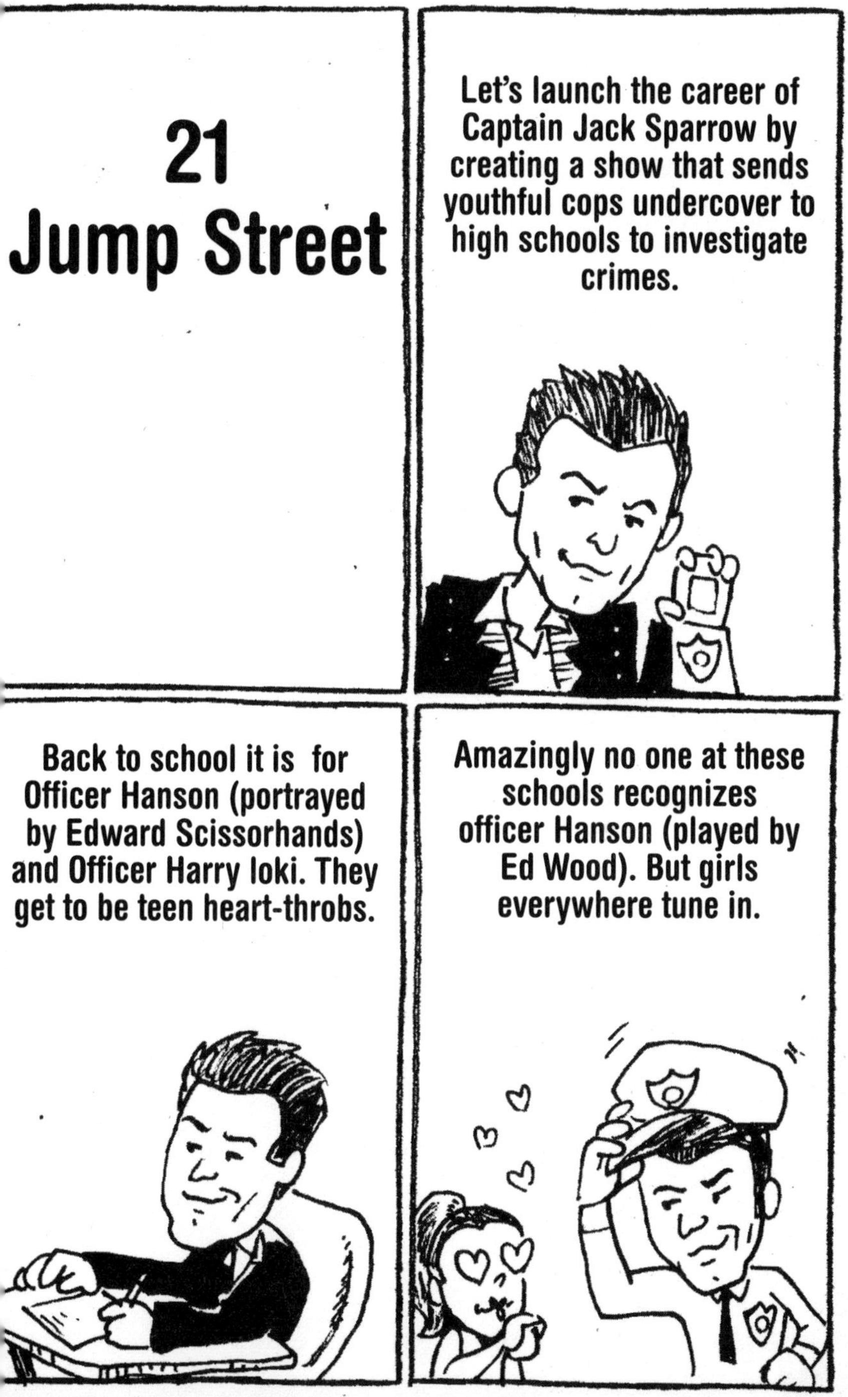
21 Jump Street
Let's launch the career of Captain Jack Sparrow by creating a show that sends youthful cops undercover to high schools to investigate crimes.
Back to school it is for Officer Hanson (portrayed by Edward Scissorhands) and Officer Harry Ioki. They get to be teen heart-throbs.
Amazingly no one at these schools recognizes officer Hanson (played by Ed Wood). But girls everywhere tune in.

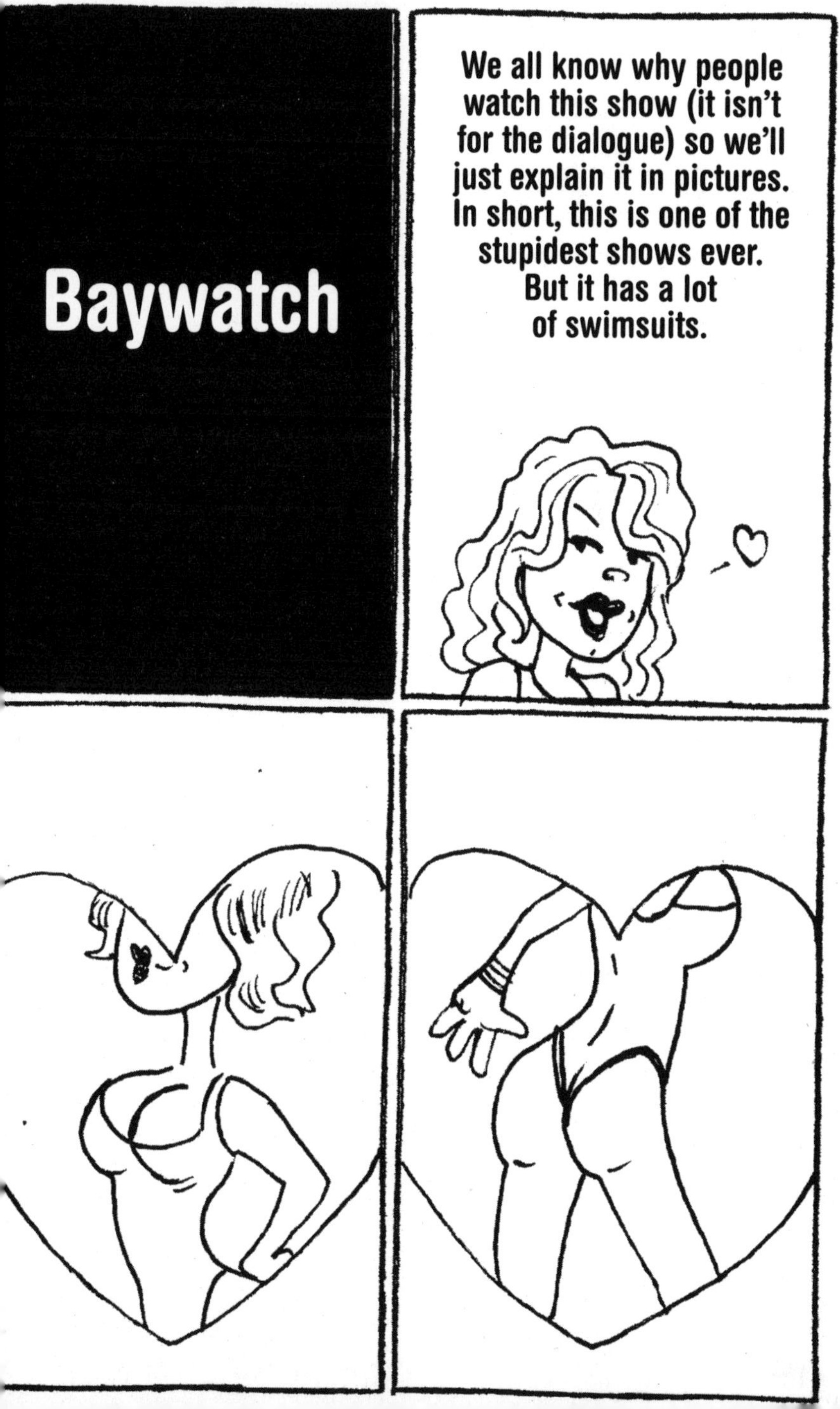
Baywatch
We all know why people watch this show (it isn't for the dialogue) so we'll just explain it in pictures. In short, this is one of the stupidest shows ever. But it has a lot of swimsuits.

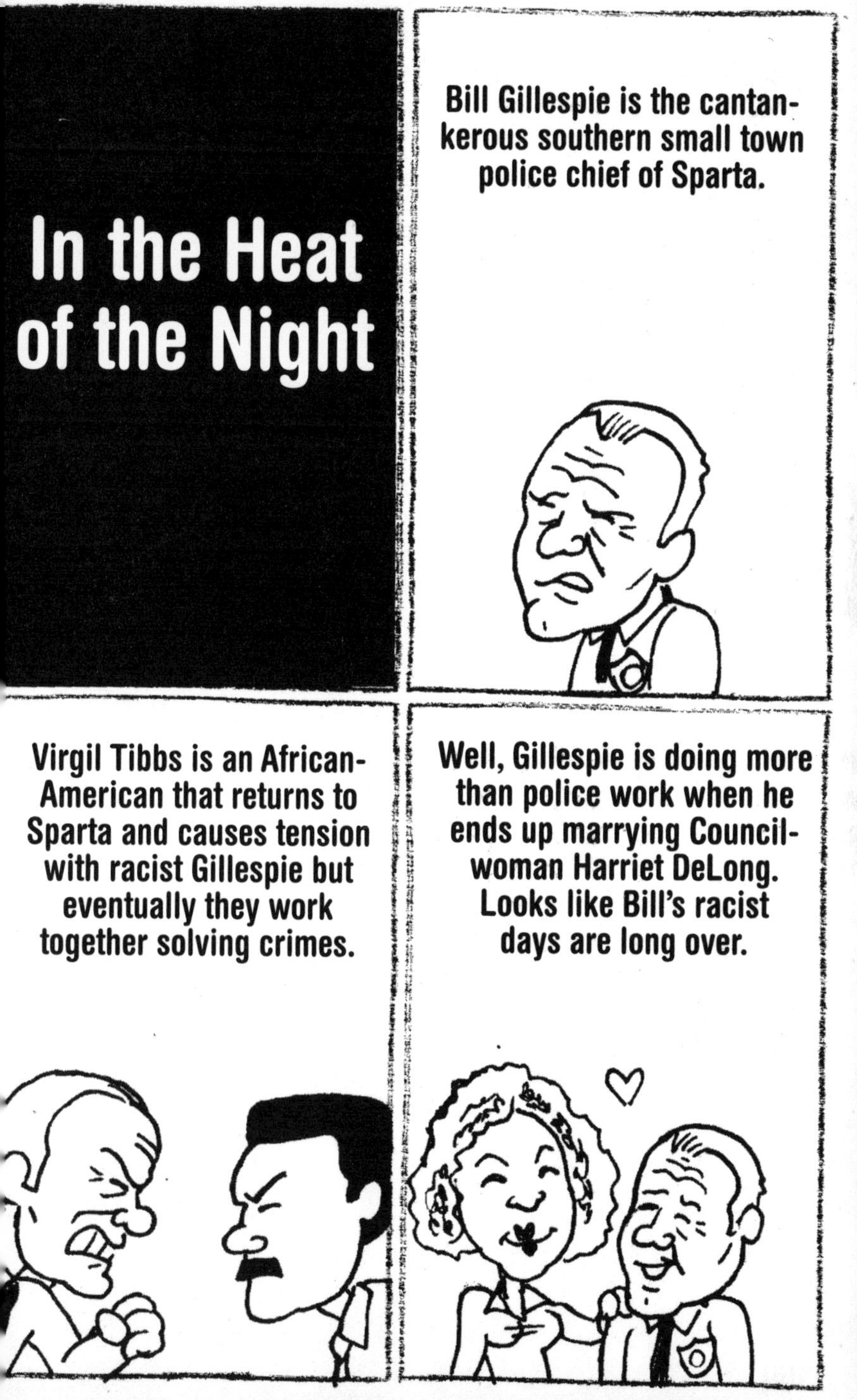
In the Heat of the Night
Bill Gillespie is the cantankerous southern small town police chief of Sparta.
Virgil Tibbs is an African-American that returns to Sparta and causes tension with racist Gillespie but eventually they work together solving crimes.
Well, Gillespie is doing more than police work when he ends up marrying Councilwoman Harriet DeLong. Looks like Bill's racist days are long over.

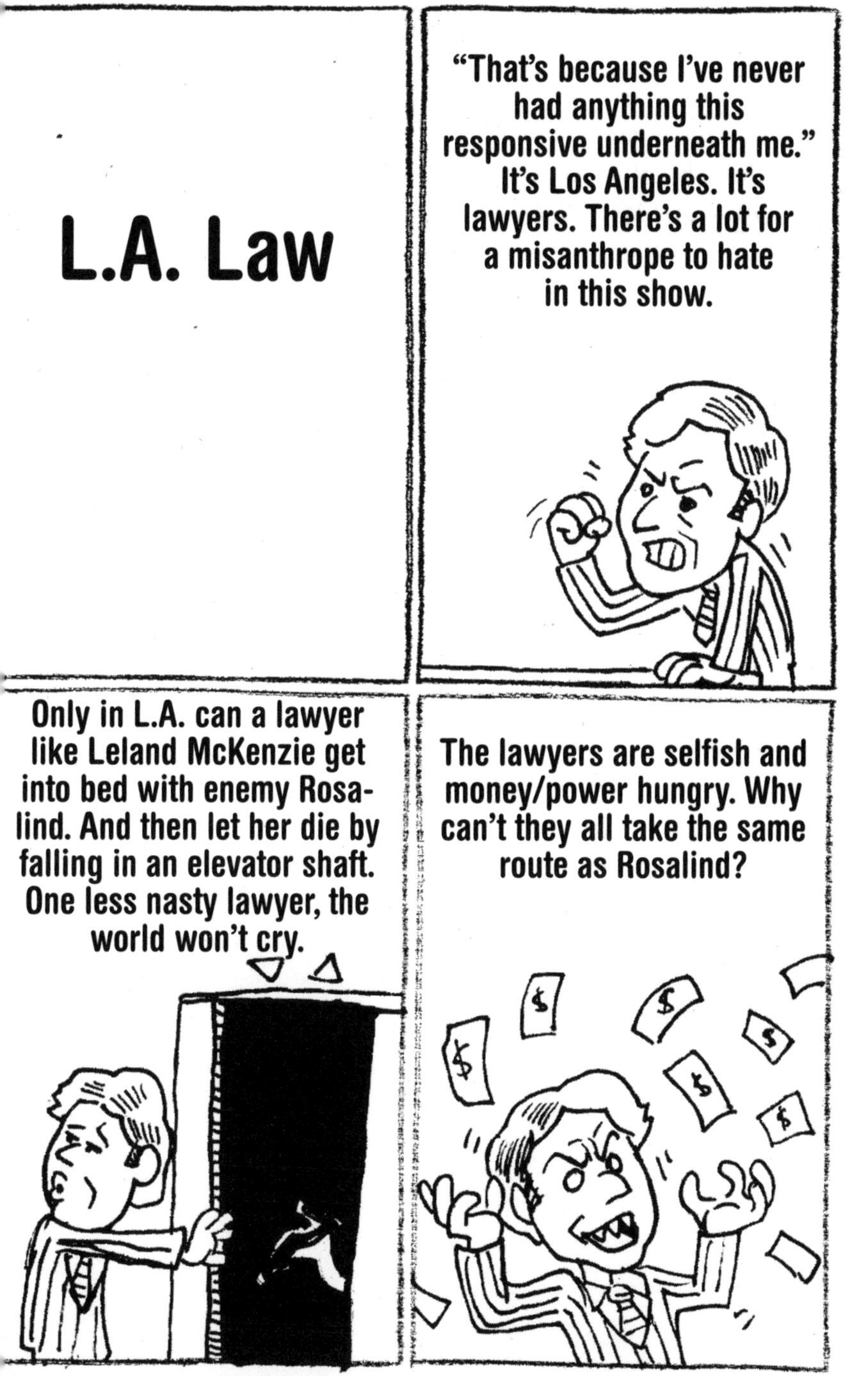
L.A. Law
"That's because I've never had anything this responsive underneath me." It's Los Angeles. It's lawyers. There's a lot for a misanthrope to hate in this show.
Only in L.A. can a lawyer like Leland McKenzie get into bed with enemy Rosalind. And then let her die by falling in an elevator shaft. One less nasty lawyer, the world won't cry.
The lawyers are selfish and money/power hungry. Why can't they all take the same route as Rosalind?

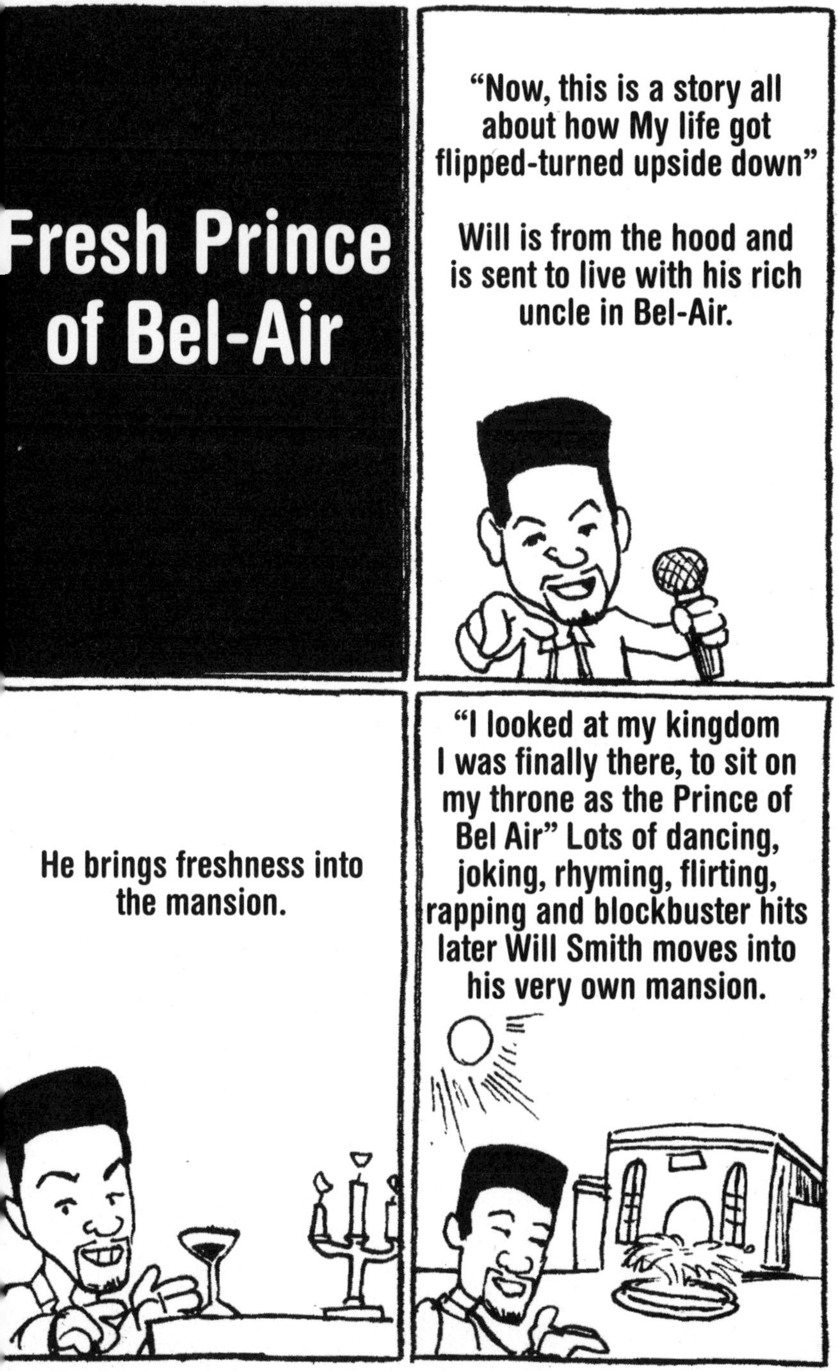
Fresh Prince of Bel-Air
"Now, this is a story all about how My life got flipped-turned upside down"
Will is from the hood and is sent to live with his rich uncle in Bel-Air.
He brings freshness into the mansion.
"I looked at my kingdom I was finally there, to sit on my throne as the Prince of Bel Air" Lots of dancing, joking, rhyming, flirting, rapping and blockbuster hits later Will Smith moves into his very own mansion.

Spin City

"Mike, look out that window. We preside over the greatest city in the world." Mike: "Sir, that's New Jersey."

Mike Flaherty runs Mayor Winston's office in New York City. Winston ain't always the sharpest knife in the drawer.

"By 9.30, well, something had built up. Let's call it... tension. And you know me... I'm a problem solver!" "Oh... Mike!" But Mike has to manage the city and has trouble managing his own life.

"Sir. You called me Charlie!" "Ah, don't let it go to your head, Mike!"

Mike had to leave for Washington so Charlie takes over his job. The clueless mayor still keeps the public fooled.

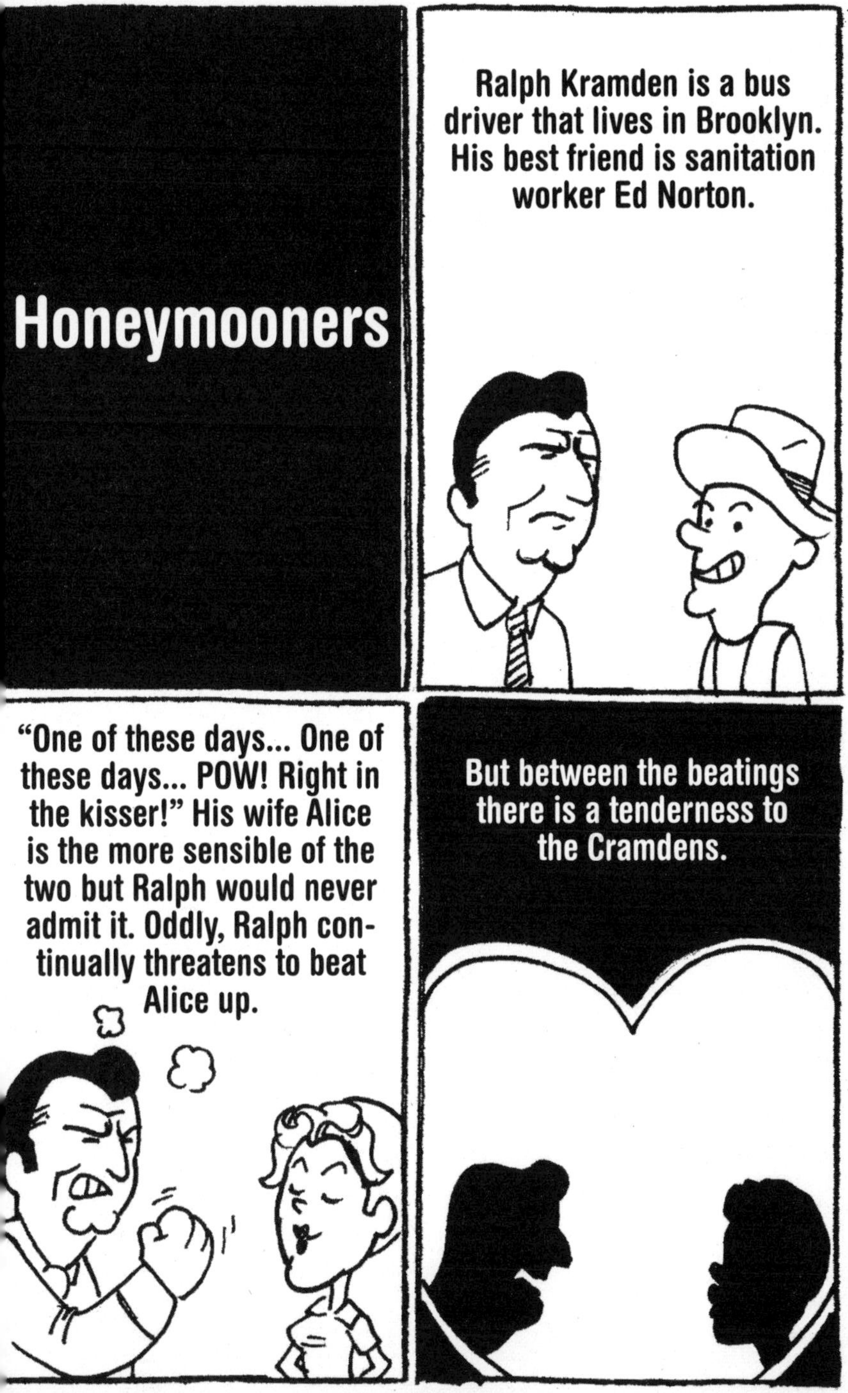
Honeymooners
Ralph Kramden is a bus driver that lives in Brooklyn. His best friend is sanitation worker Ed Norton.
"One of these days... One of these days... POW! Right in the kisser!" His wife Alice is the more sensible of the two but Ralph would never admit it. Oddly, Ralph continually threatens to beat Alice up.
But between the beatings there is a tenderness to the Cramdens.

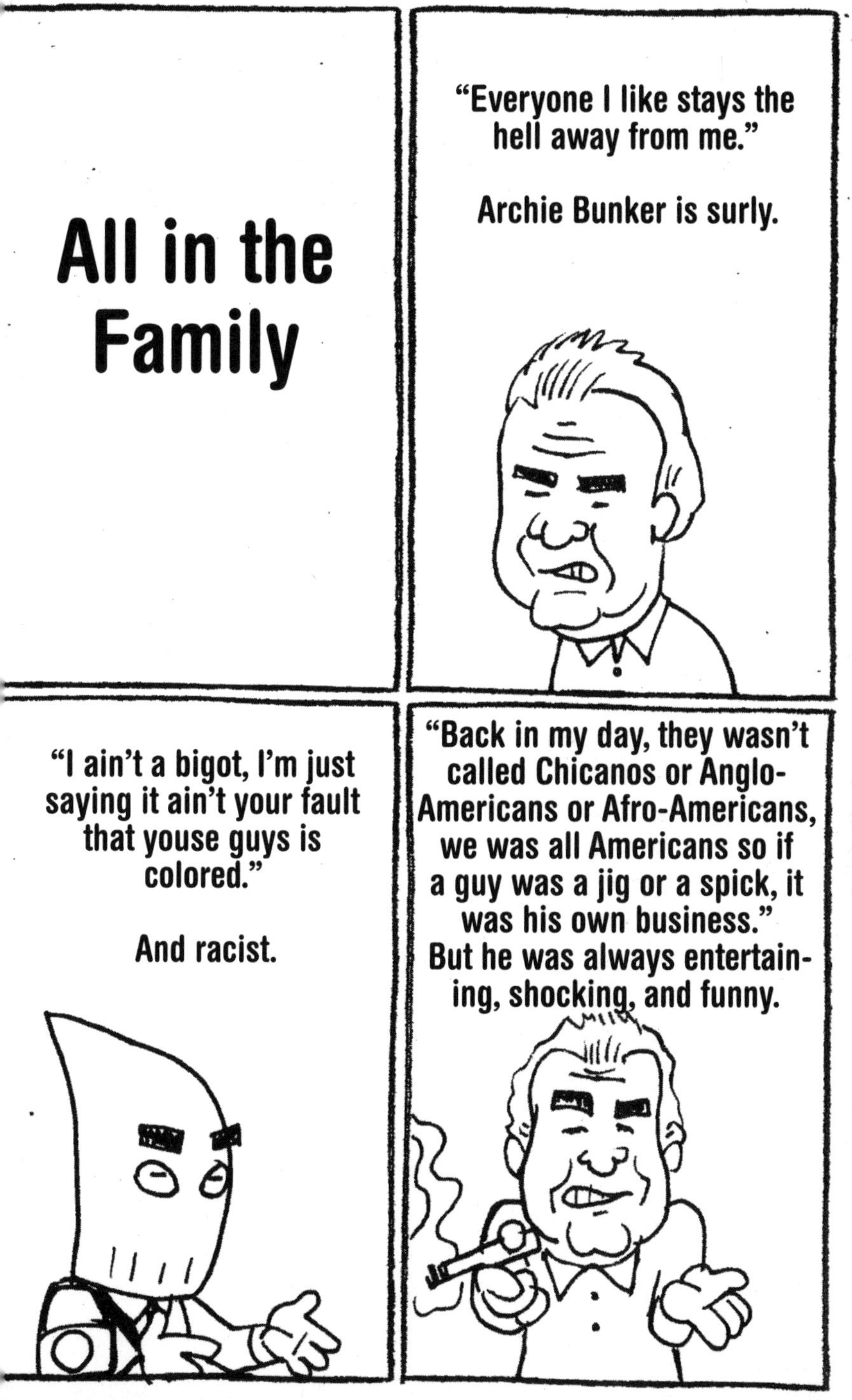
All in the Family
"Everyone I like stays the hell away from me."
Archie Bunker is surly.
"I ain't a bigot, I'm just saying it ain't your fault that youse guys is colored."
And racist.
"Back in my day, they wasn't called Chicanos or Anglo-Americans or Afro-Americans, we was all Americans so if a guy was a jig or a spick, it was his own business."
But he was always entertaining, shocking, and funny.

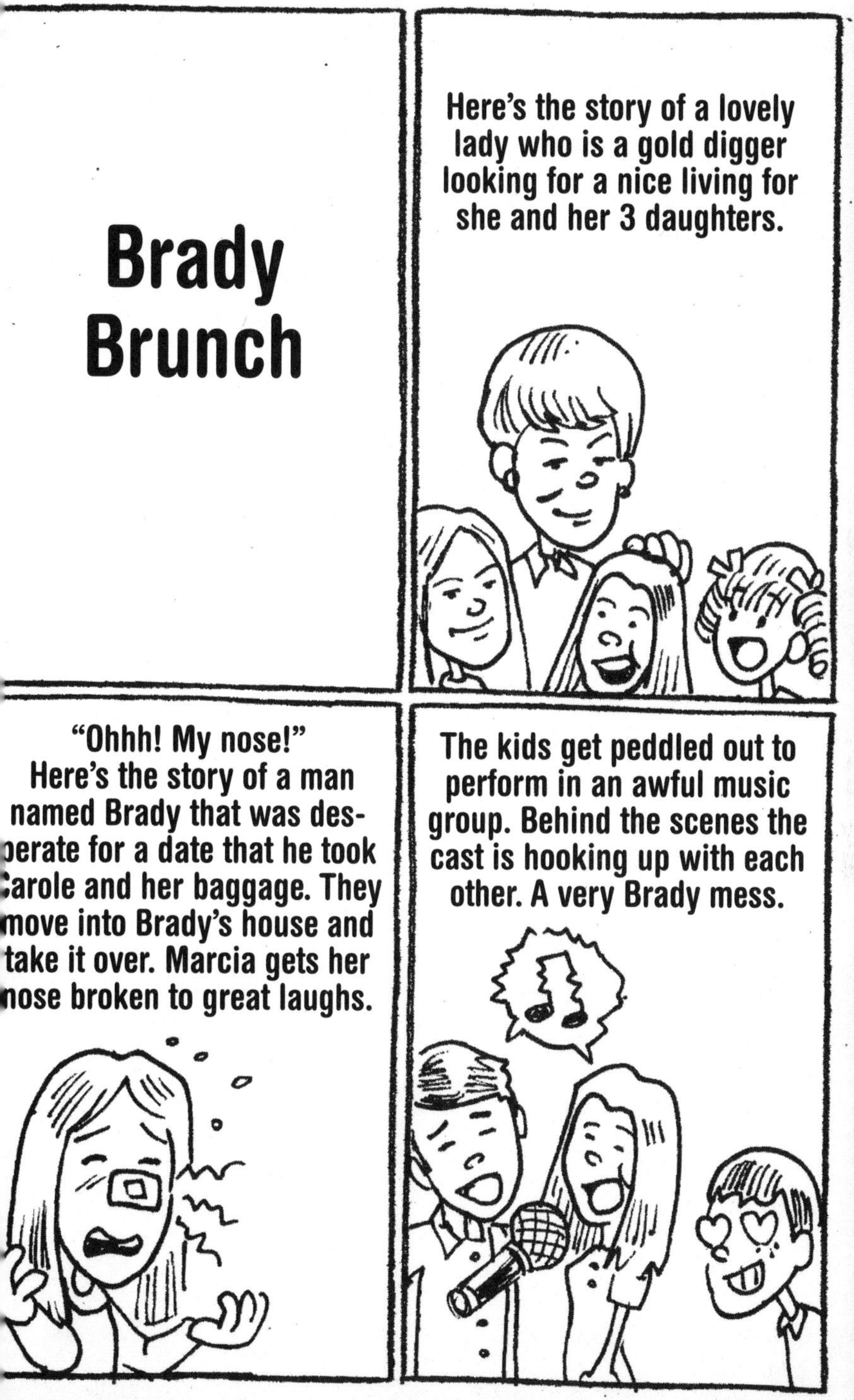
Brady Brunch
Here's the story of a lovely lady who is a gold digger looking for a nice living for she and her 3 daughters.
"Ohhh! My nose!"
Here's the story of a man named Brady that was desperate for a date that he took Carole and her baggage. They move into Brady's house and take it over. Marcia gets her nose broken to great laughs.
The kids get peddled out to perform in an awful music group. Behind the scenes the cast is hooking up with each other. A very Brady mess.

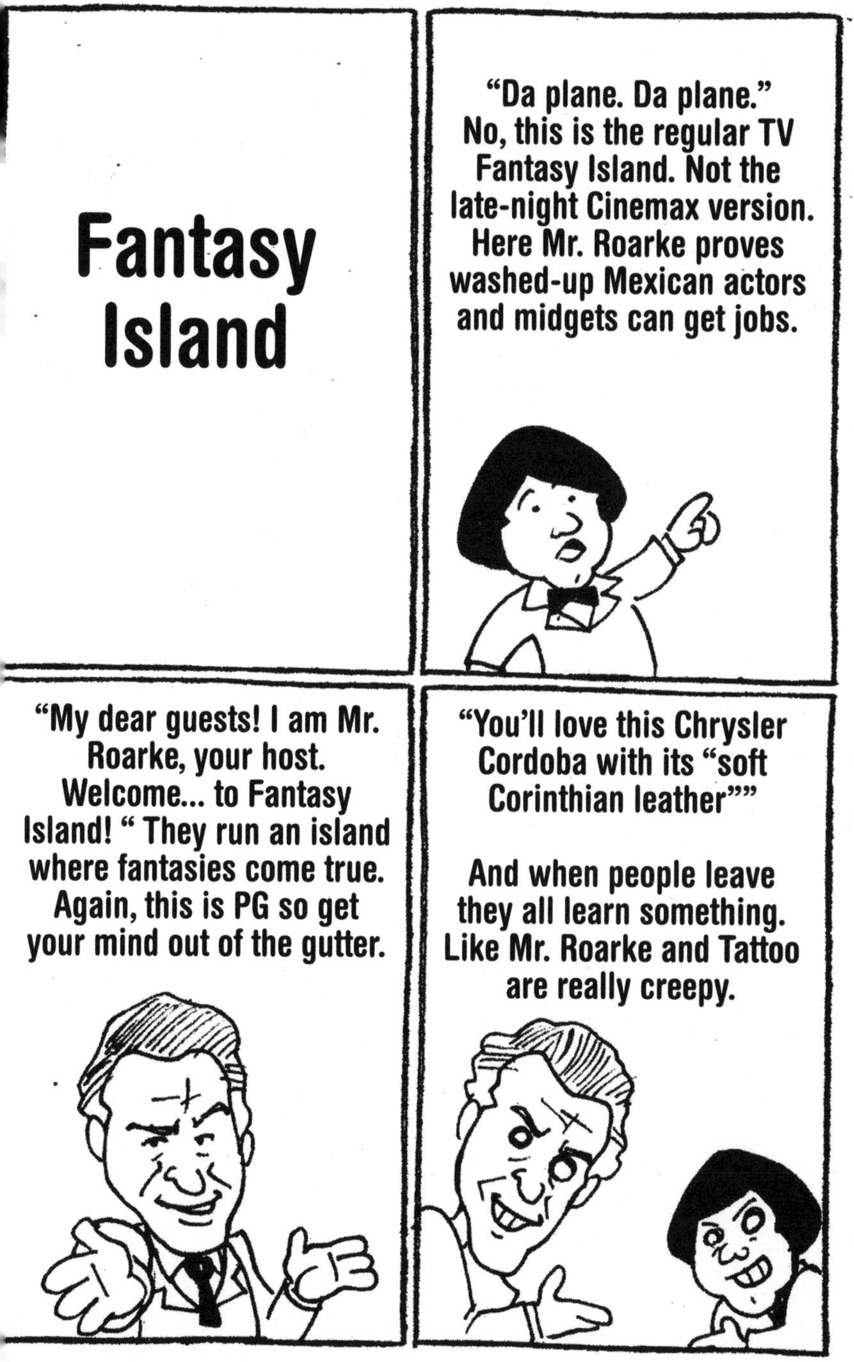
Fantasy Island
"Da plane. Da plane." No, this is the regular TV Fantasy Island. Not the late-night Cinemax version. Here Mr. Roarke proves washed-up Mexican actors and midgets can get jobs.
"My dear guests! I am Mr. Roarke, your host. Welcome... to Fantasy Island! " They run an island where fantasies come true. Again, this is PG so get your mind out of the gutter.
"You'll love this Chrysler Cordoba with its "soft Corinthian leather""
And when people leave they all learn something. Like Mr. Roarke and Tattoo are really creepy.

Leave it to Beaver

The Cleavers live in Mayfield. The two sons, Wally and Theodore (Beaver) skip through life happily. With a nickname like Beaver you wonder how. He'll deal with issues in therapy later in life.

Mr. and Mrs. Cleaver are the all American parents. They don't get angry and teach their kids values. They're probably stoned.

"Wally, if your dumb brother tags along, I'm gonna - oh, good afternoon, Mrs. Cleaver. I was just telling Wallace how pleasant it would be for Theodore to accompany us to the movies." Wally's friend Eddie Haskell inspires kids to lie and brownnose adults everywhere. He rules.

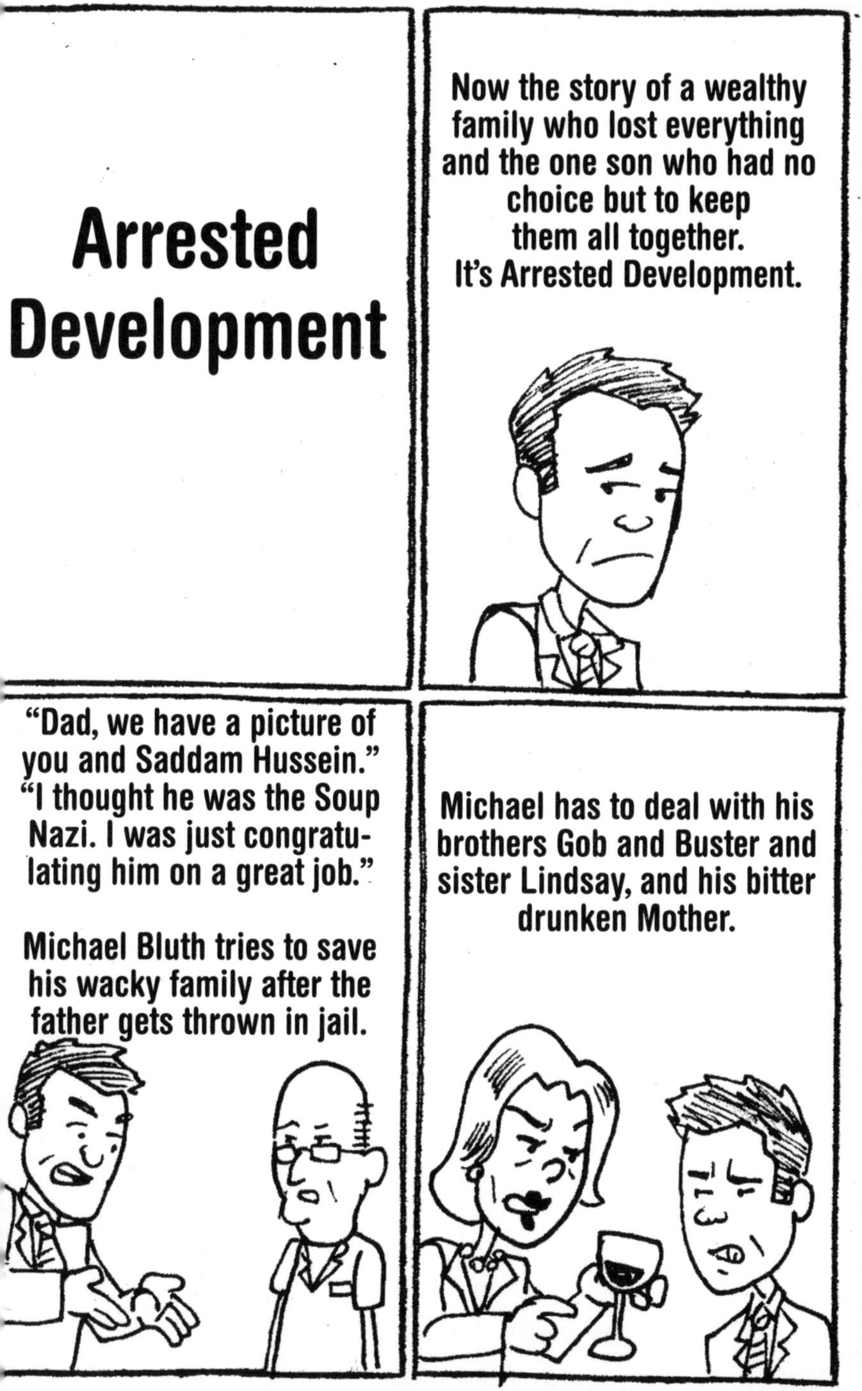
Arrested Development
Now the story of a wealthy family who lost everything and the one son who had no choice but to keep them all together. It's Arrested Development.
"Dad, we have a picture of you and Saddam Hussein." "I thought he was the Soup Nazi. I was just congratulating him on a great job."
Michael Bluth tries to save his wacky family after the father gets thrown in jail.
Michael has to deal with his brothers Gob and Buster and sister Lindsay, and his bitter drunken Mother.

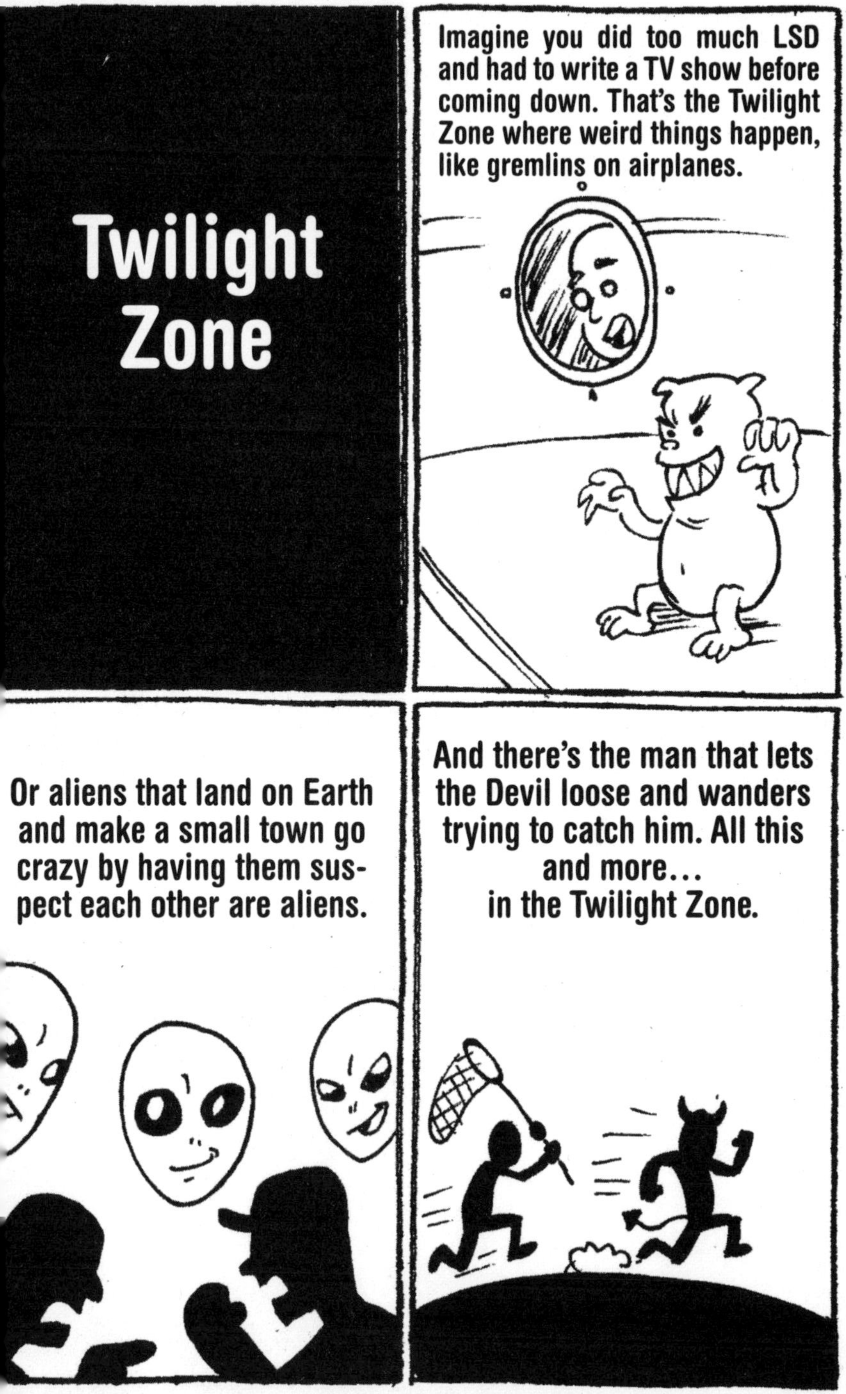
Twilight Zone
Imagine you did too much LSD and had to write a TV show before coming down. That's the Twilight Zone where weird things happen, like gremlins on airplanes.
Or aliens that land on Earth and make a small town go crazy by having them suspect each other are aliens.
And there's the man that lets the Devil loose and wanders trying to catch him. All this and more…
in the Twilight Zone.

I Love Lucy

Lucy and Desi love each other but sleep in separate beds. Television was different back then.

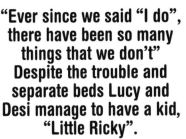

"Luuuucy"

ucy gets into trouble trying o get into show business. si gets camera time getting gry. Fred and Ethel play the sidekicks.

"Ever since we said "I do", there have been so many things that we don't" Despite the trouble and separate beds Lucy and Desi manage to have a kid, "Little Ricky".

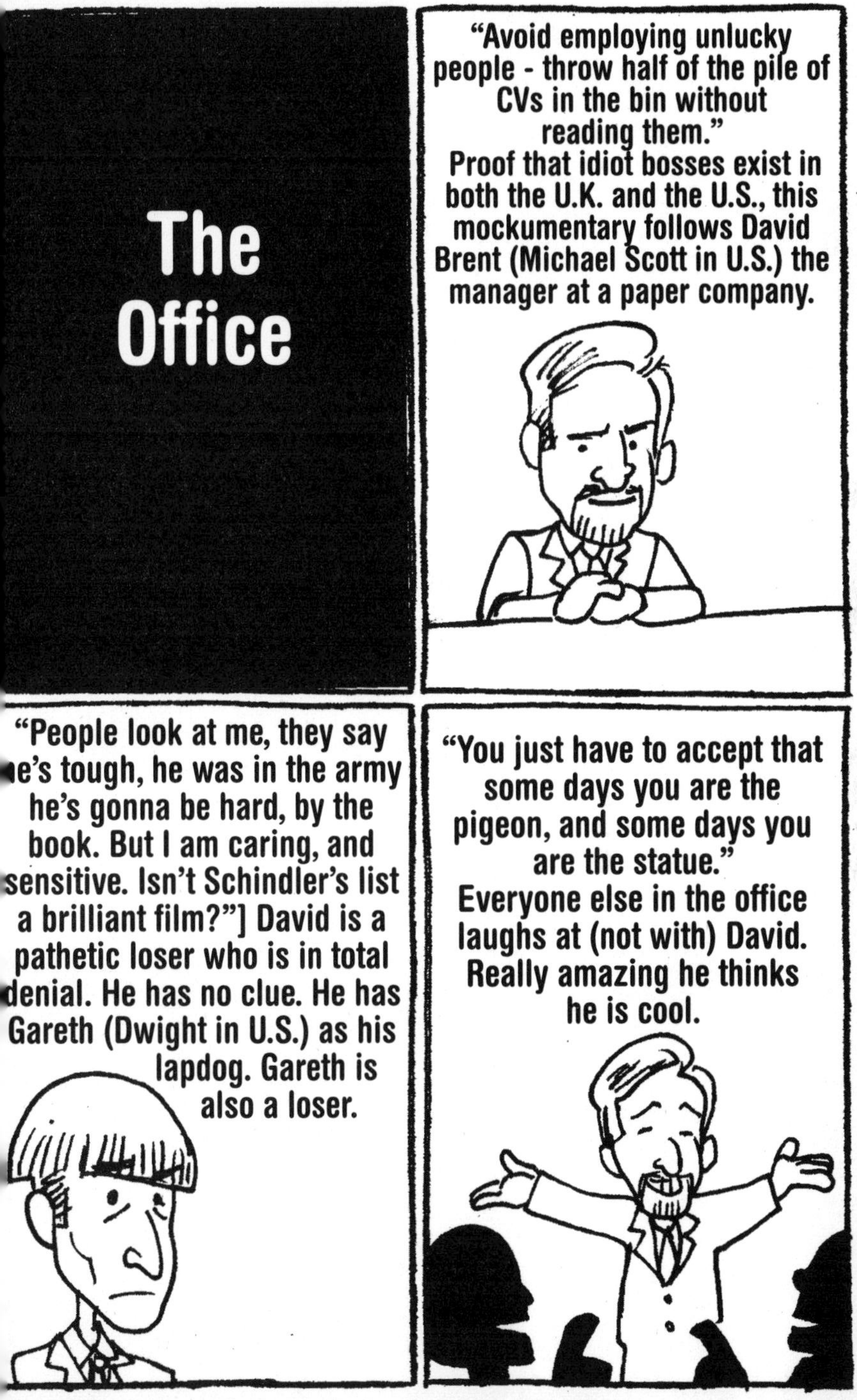
The Office
"Avoid employing unlucky people - throw half of the pile of CVs in the bin without reading them."
Proof that idiot bosses exist in both the U.K. and the U.S., this mockumentary follows David Brent (Michael Scott in U.S.) the manager at a paper company.
"People look at me, they say e's tough, he was in the army he's gonna be hard, by the book. But I am caring, and sensitive. Isn't Schindler's list a brilliant film?"] David is a pathetic loser who is in total denial. He has no clue. He has Gareth (Dwight in U.S.) as his lapdog. Gareth is also a loser.
"You just have to accept that some days you are the pigeon, and some days you are the statue."
Everyone else in the office laughs at (not with) David. Really amazing he thinks he is cool.

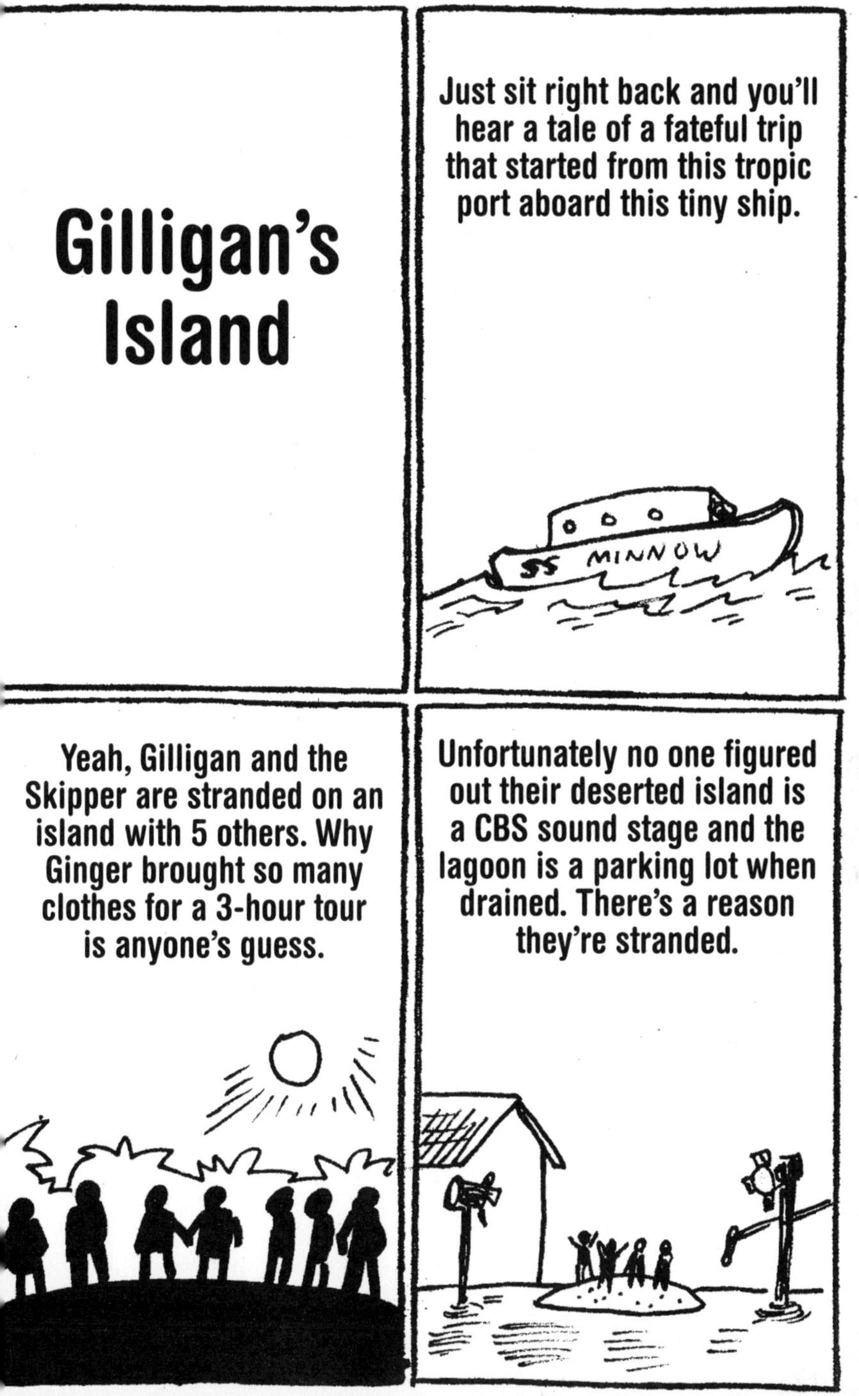
Gilligan's Island
Just sit right back and you'll hear a tale of a fateful trip that started from this tropic port aboard this tiny ship.
SS MINNOW
Yeah, Gilligan and the Skipper are stranded on an island with 5 others. Why Ginger brought so many clothes for a 3-hour tour is anyone's guess.
Unfortunately no one figured out their deserted island is a CBS sound stage and the lagoon is a parking lot when drained. There's a reason they're stranded.

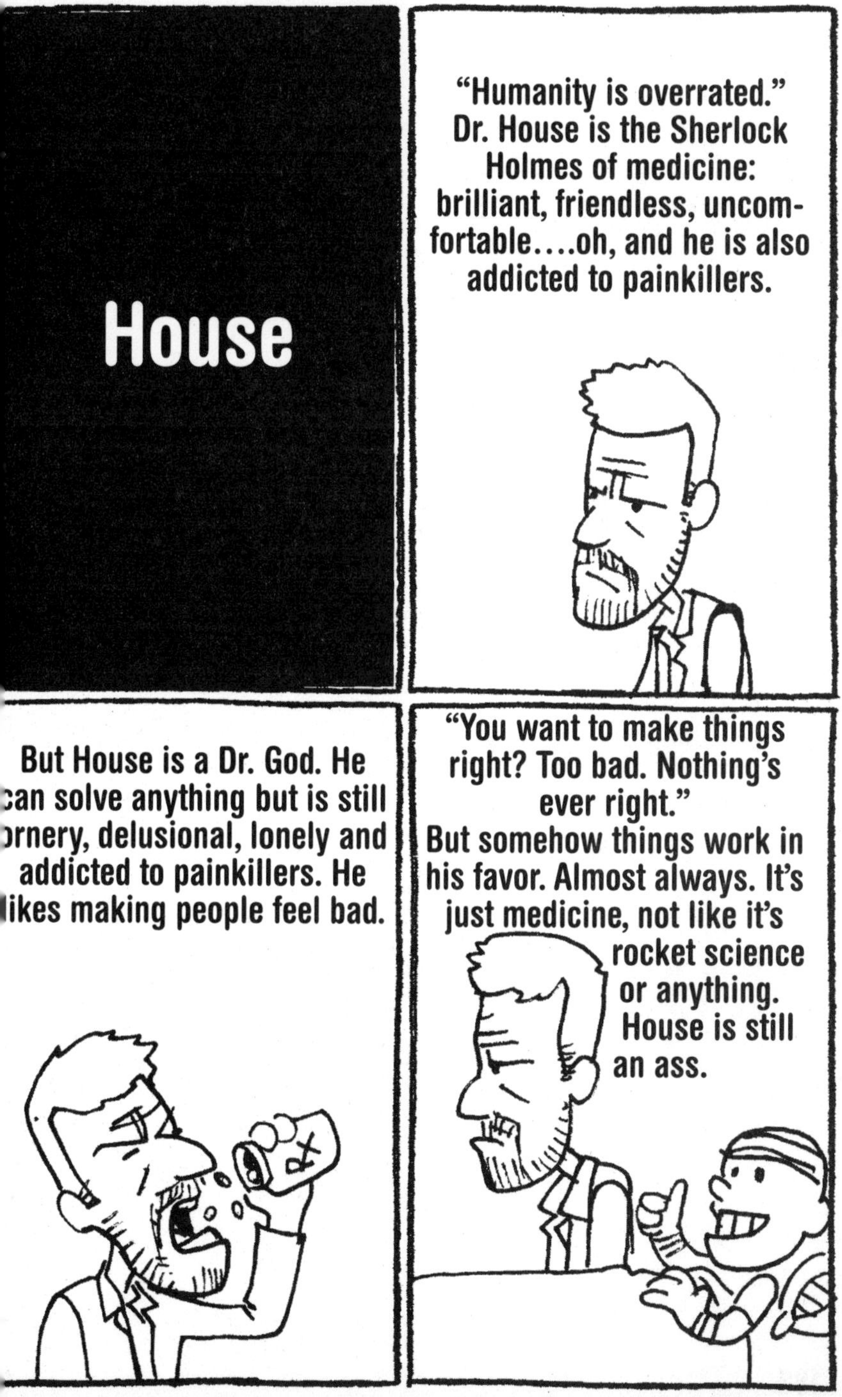
House
"Humanity is overrated." Dr. House is the Sherlock Holmes of medicine: brilliant, friendless, uncom-fortable....oh, and he is also addicted to painkillers.
But House is a Dr. God. He can solve anything but is still ornery, delusional, lonely and addicted to painkillers. He likes making people feel bad.
Rx
"You want to make things right? Too bad. Nothing's ever right."
But somehow things work in his favor. Almost always. It's just medicine, not like it's rocket science or anything. House is still an ass.

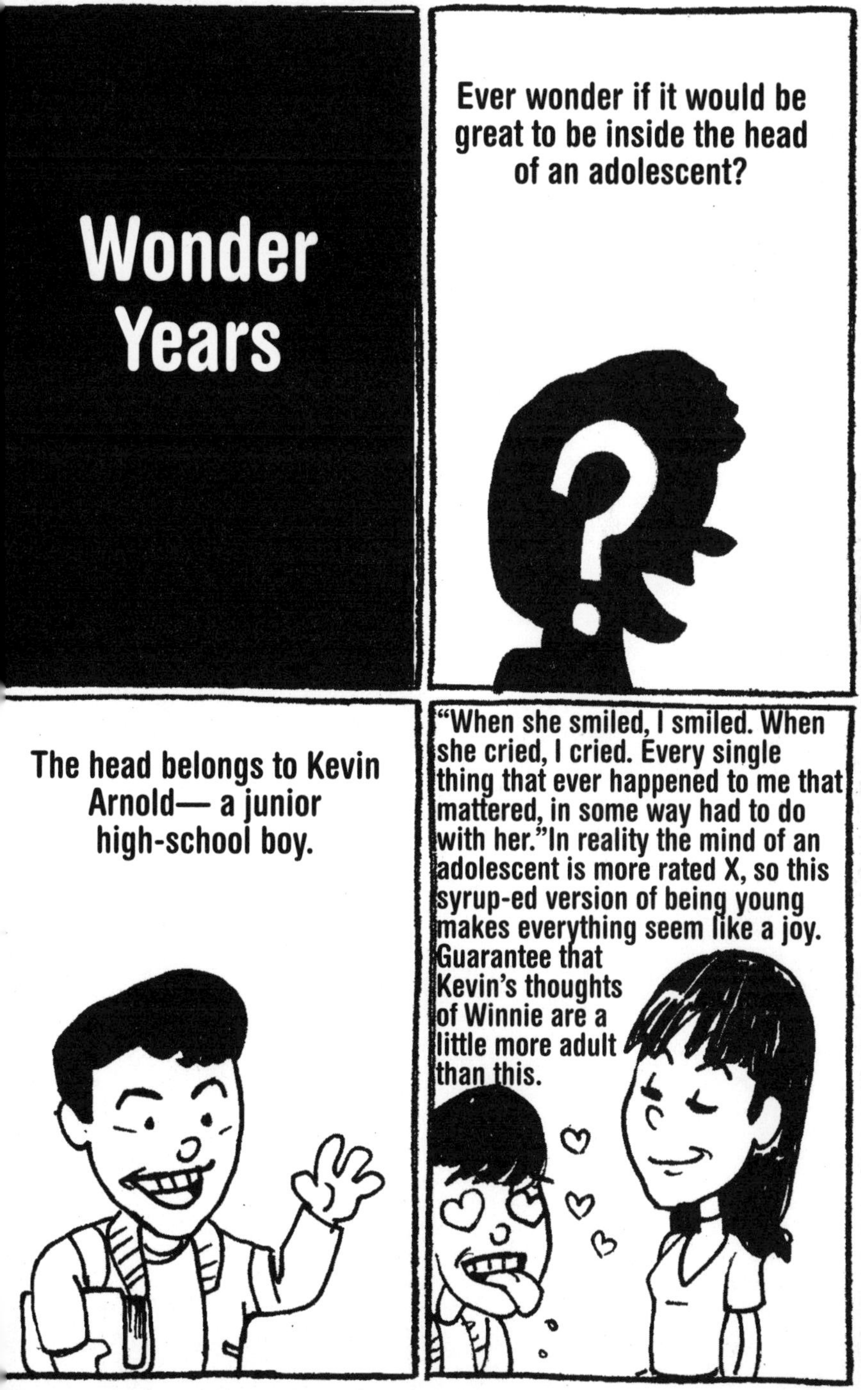
Wonder Years
Ever wonder if it would be great to be inside the head of an adolescent?
The head belongs to Kevin Arnold— a junior high-school boy.
"When she smiled, I smiled. When she cried, I cried. Every single thing that ever happened to me that mattered, in some way had to do with her."In reality the mind of an adolescent is more rated X, so this syrup-ed version of being young makes everything seem like a joy.
Guarantee that Kevin's thoughts of Winnie are a little more adult than this.

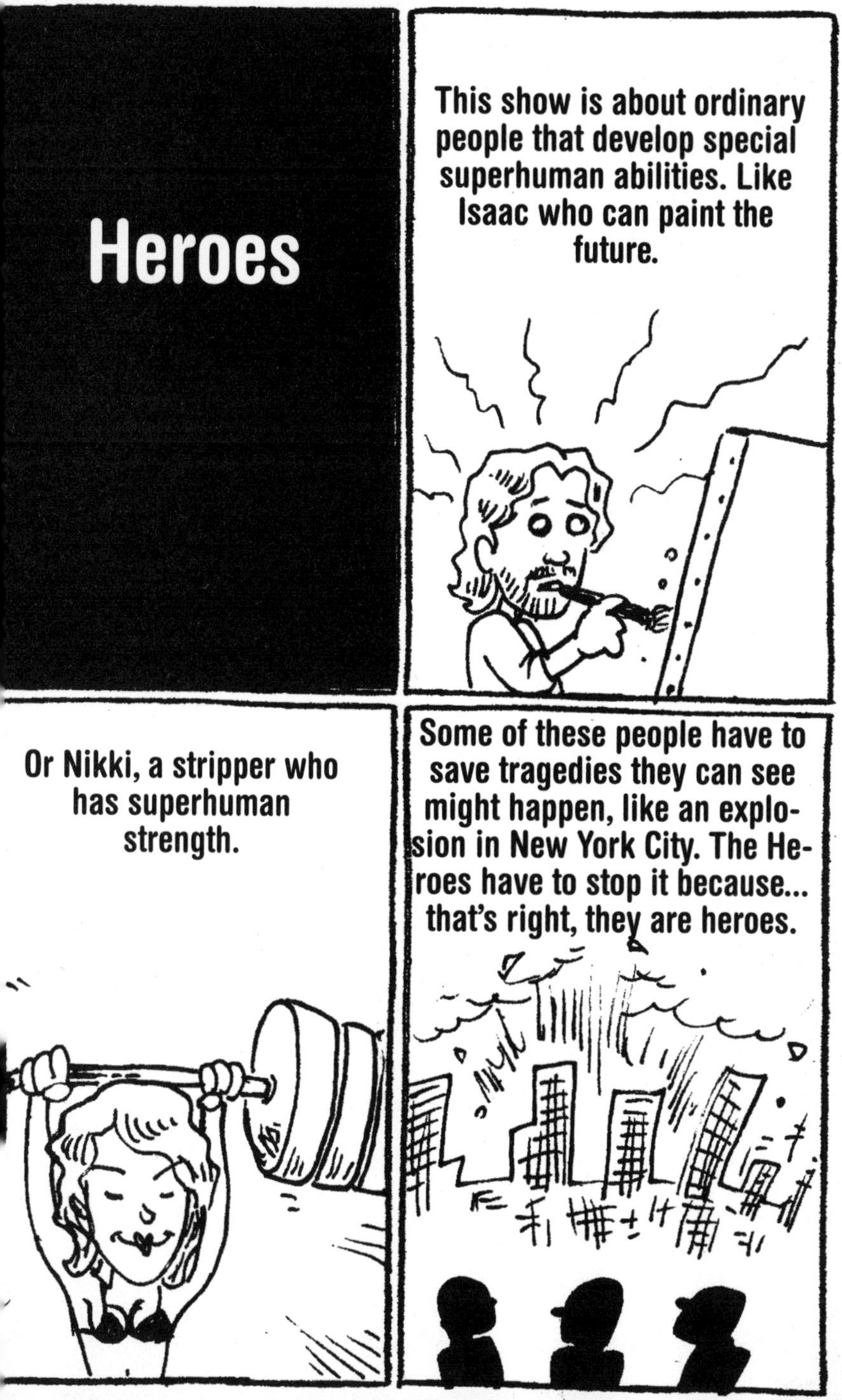
Heroes
This show is about ordinary people that develop special superhuman abilities. Like Isaac who can paint the future.
Or Nikki, a stripper who has superhuman strength.
Some of these people have to save tragedies they can see might happen, like an explosion in New York City. The Heroes have to stop it because... that's right, they are heroes.

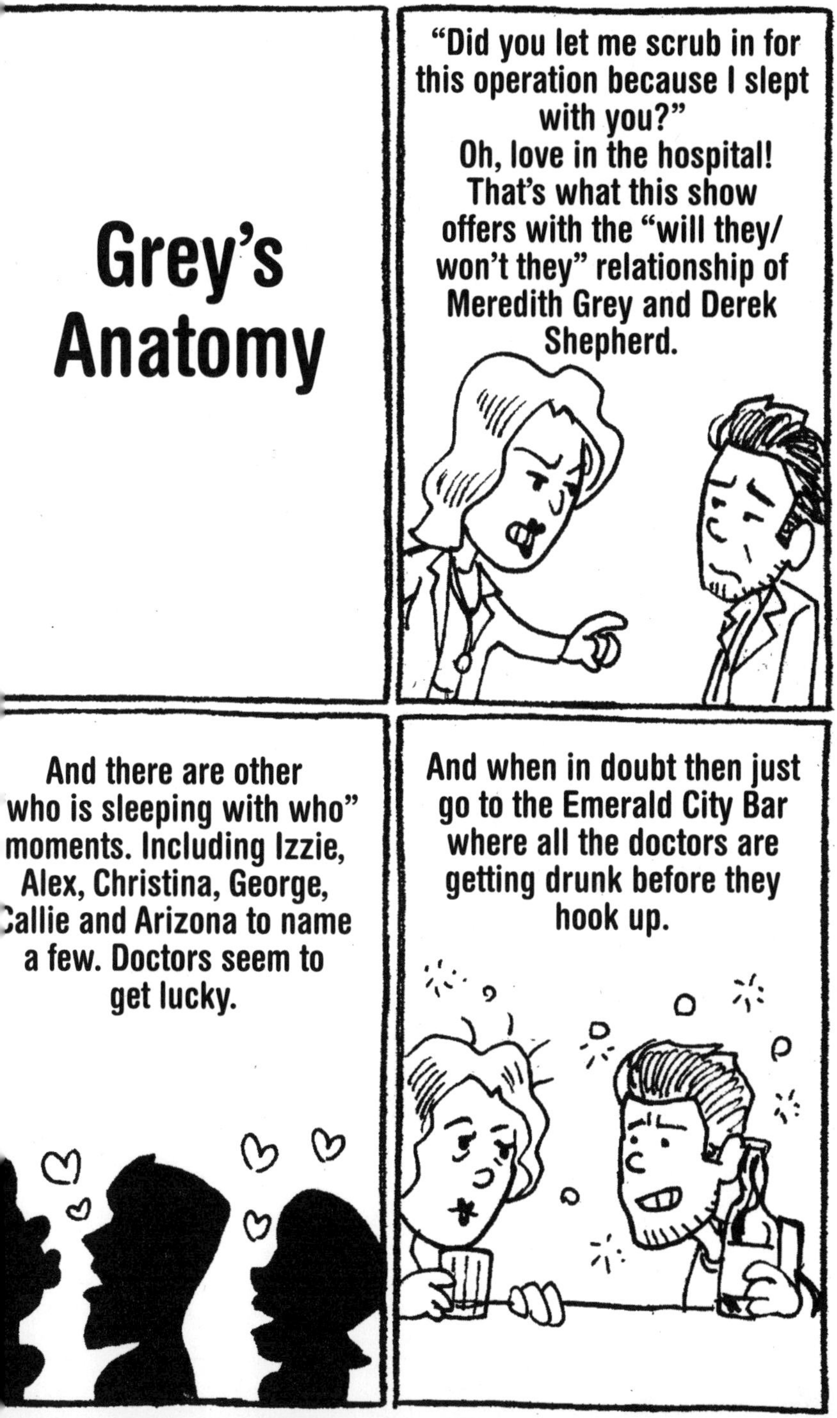
Grey’s Anatomy
“Did you let me scrub in for this operation because I slept with you?”
Oh, love in the hospital! That’s what this show offers with the “will they/ won’t they” relationship of Meredith Grey and Derek Shepherd.
And there are other who is sleeping with who” moments. Including Izzie, Alex, Christina, George, Callie and Arizona to name a few. Doctors seem to get lucky.
And when in doubt then just go to the Emerald City Bar where all the doctors are getting drunk before they hook up.

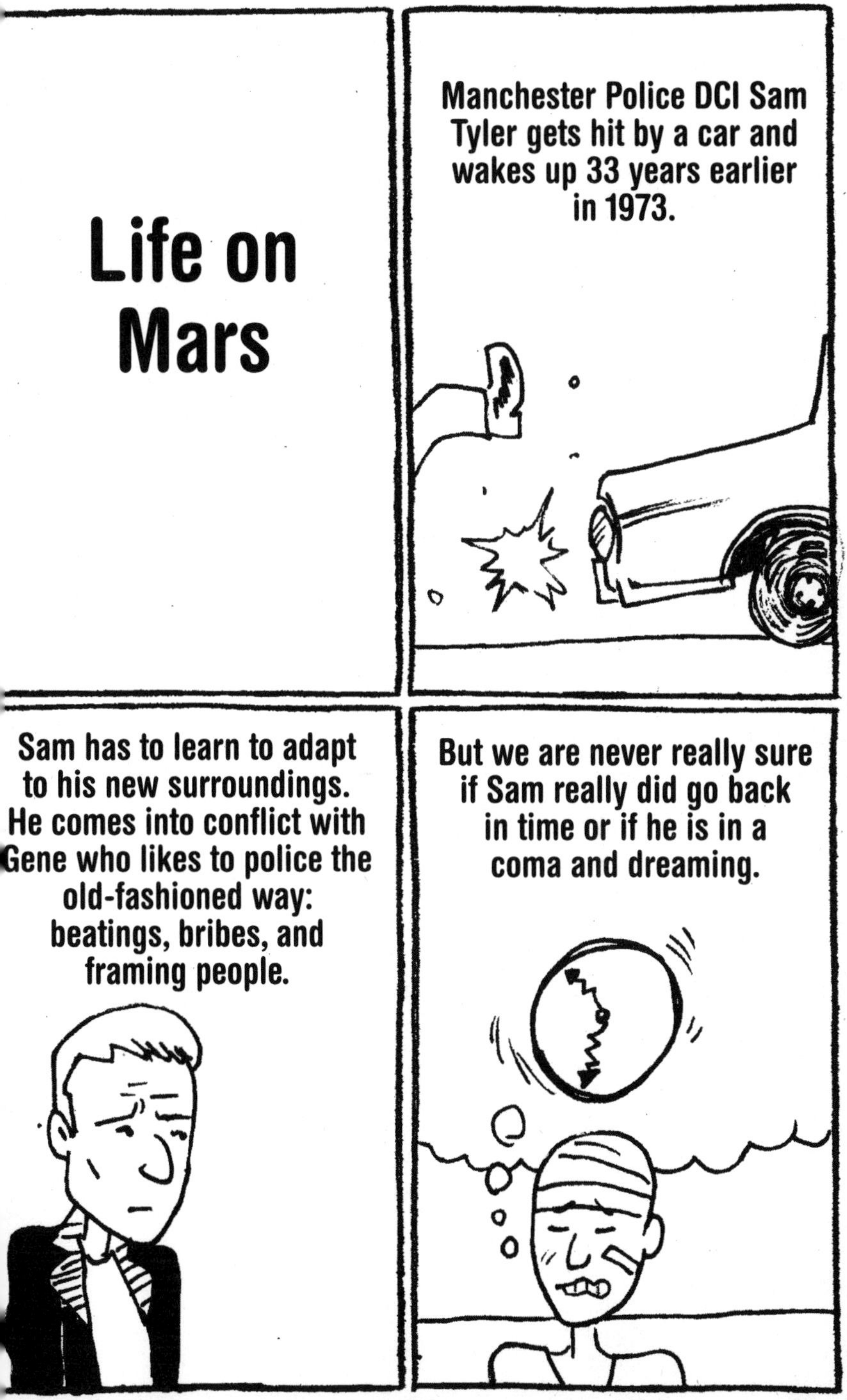
Life on Mars
Manchester Police DCI Sam Tyler gets hit by a car and wakes up 33 years earlier in 1973.
Sam has to learn to adapt to his new surroundings. He comes into conflict with Gene who likes to police the old-fashioned way: beatings, bribes, and framing people.
But we are never really sure if Sam really did go back in time or if he is in a coma and dreaming.

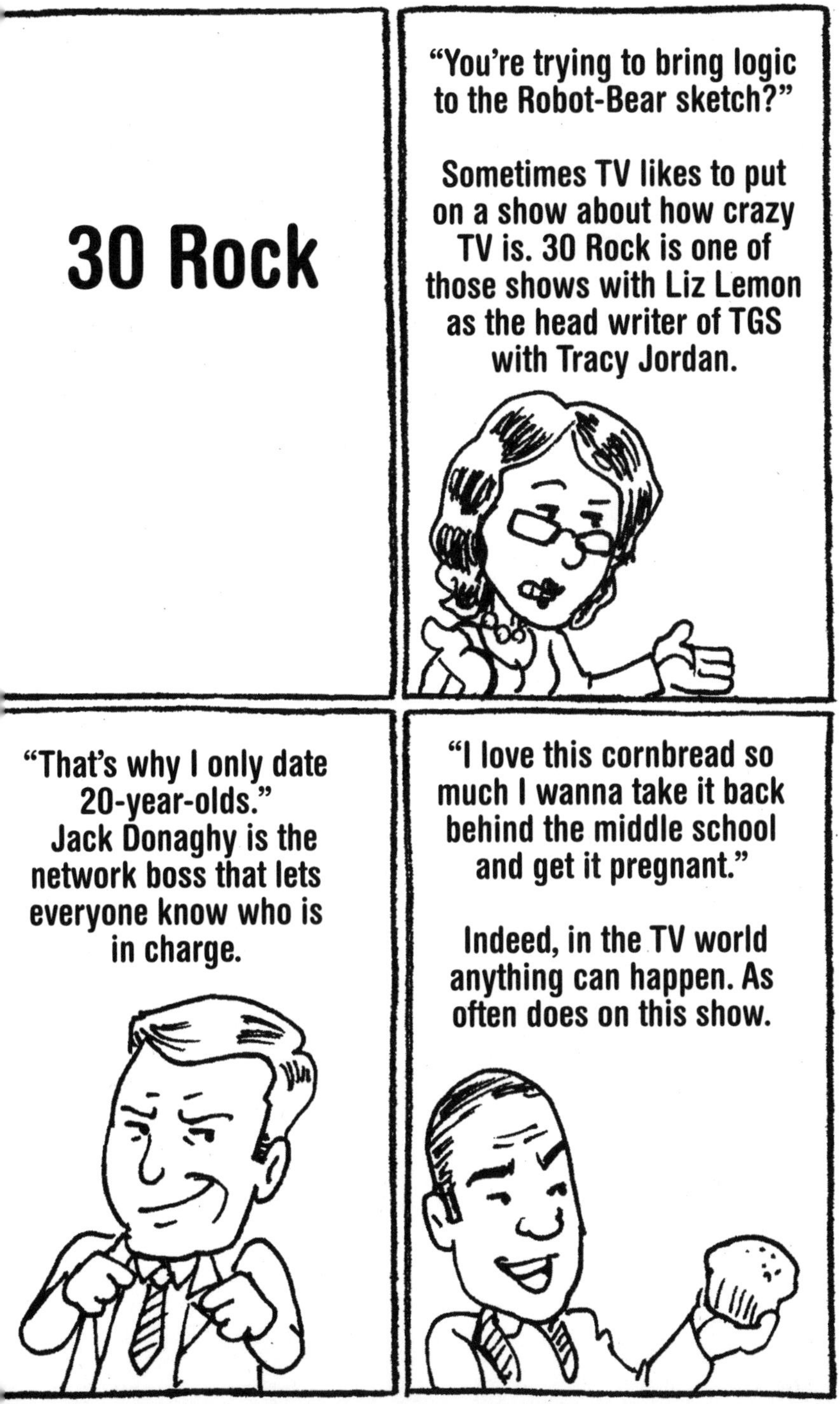
30 Rock
"You're trying to bring logic to the Robot-Bear sketch?"
Sometimes TV likes to put on a show about how crazy TV is. 30 Rock is one of those shows with Liz Lemon as the head writer of TGS with Tracy Jordan.
"That's why I only date 20-year-olds."
Jack Donaghy is the network boss that lets everyone know who is in charge.
"I love this cornbread so much I wanna take it back behind the middle school and get it pregnant."
Indeed, in the TV world anything can happen. As often does on this show.

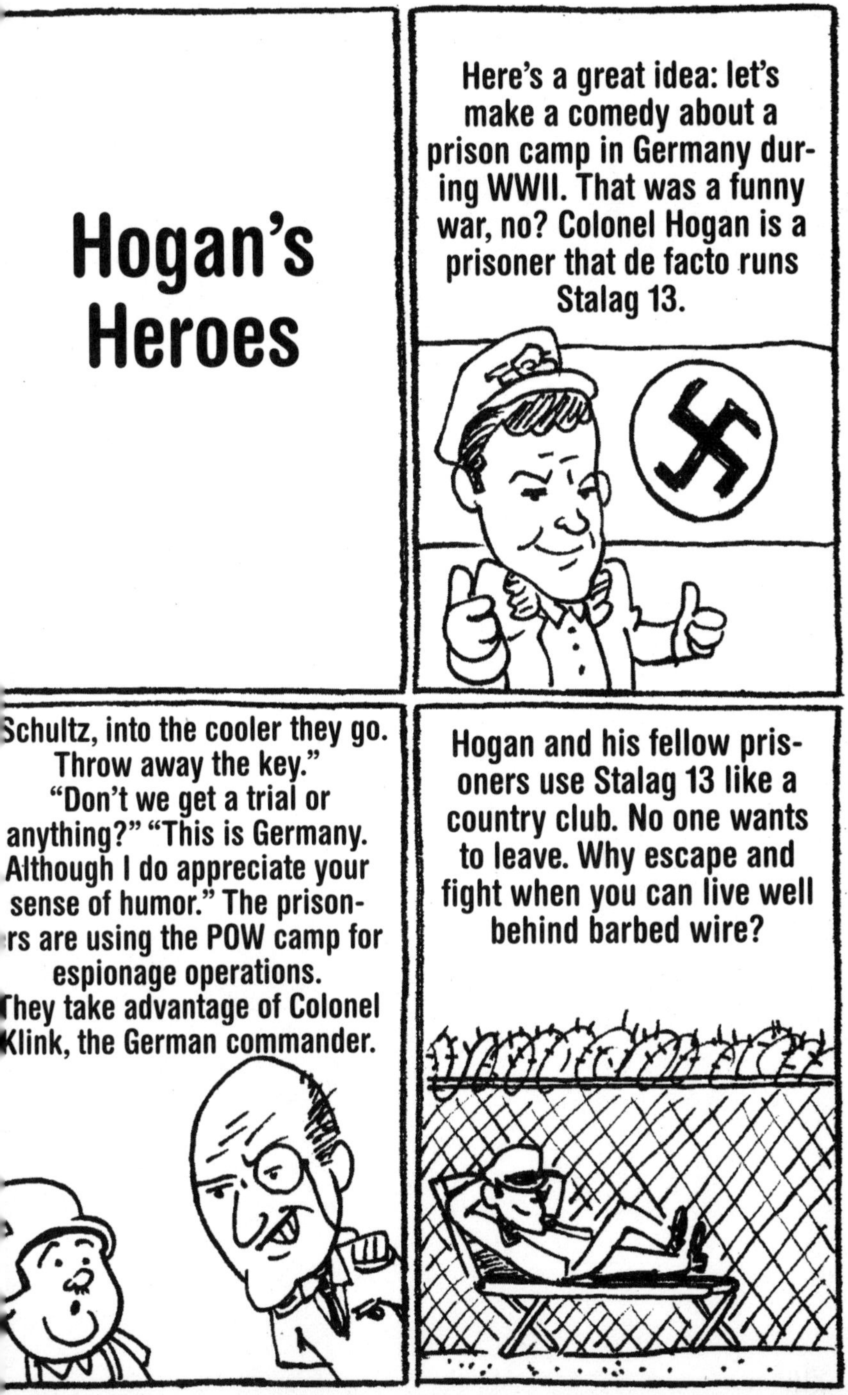
Hogan's Heroes
Here's a great idea: let's make a comedy about a prison camp in Germany during WWII. That was a funny war, no? Colonel Hogan is a prisoner that de facto runs Stalag 13.
Schultz, into the cooler they go. Throw away the key." "Don't we get a trial or anything?" "This is Germany. Although I do appreciate your sense of humor." The prisoners are using the POW camp for espionage operations. They take advantage of Colonel Klink, the German commander.
Hogan and his fellow prisoners use Stalag 13 like a country club. No one wants to leave. Why escape and fight when you can live well behind barbed wire?

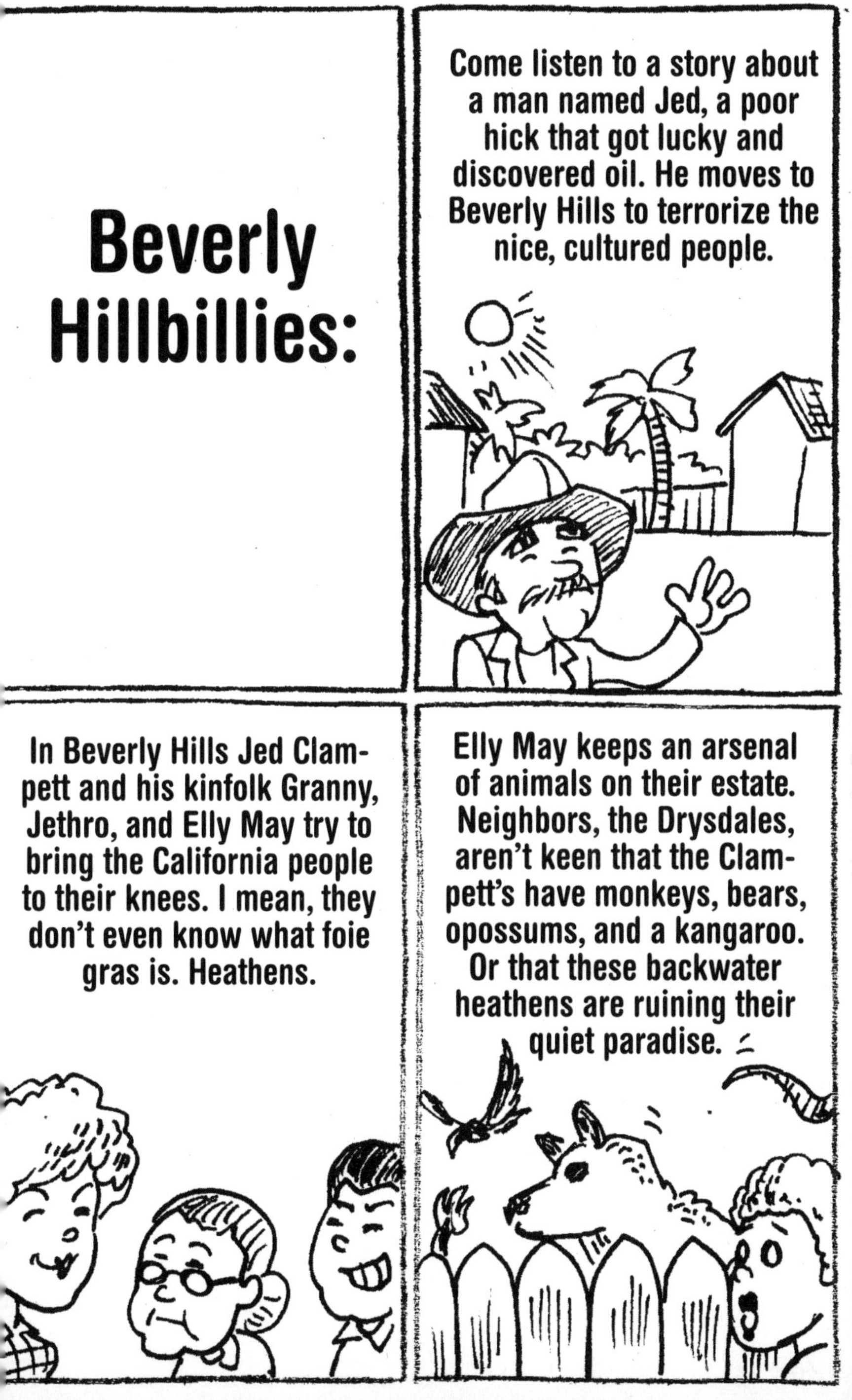
Beverly Hillbillies:
Come listen to a story about a man named Jed, a poor hick that got lucky and discovered oil. He moves to Beverly Hills to terrorize the nice, cultured people.
In Beverly Hills Jed Clampett and his kinfolk Granny, Jethro, and Elly May try to bring the California people to their knees. I mean, they don't even know what foie gras is. Heathens.
Elly May keeps an arsenal of animals on their estate. Neighbors, the Drysdales, aren't keen that the Clampett's have monkeys, bears, opossums, and a kangaroo. Or that these backwater heathens are ruining their quiet paradise.

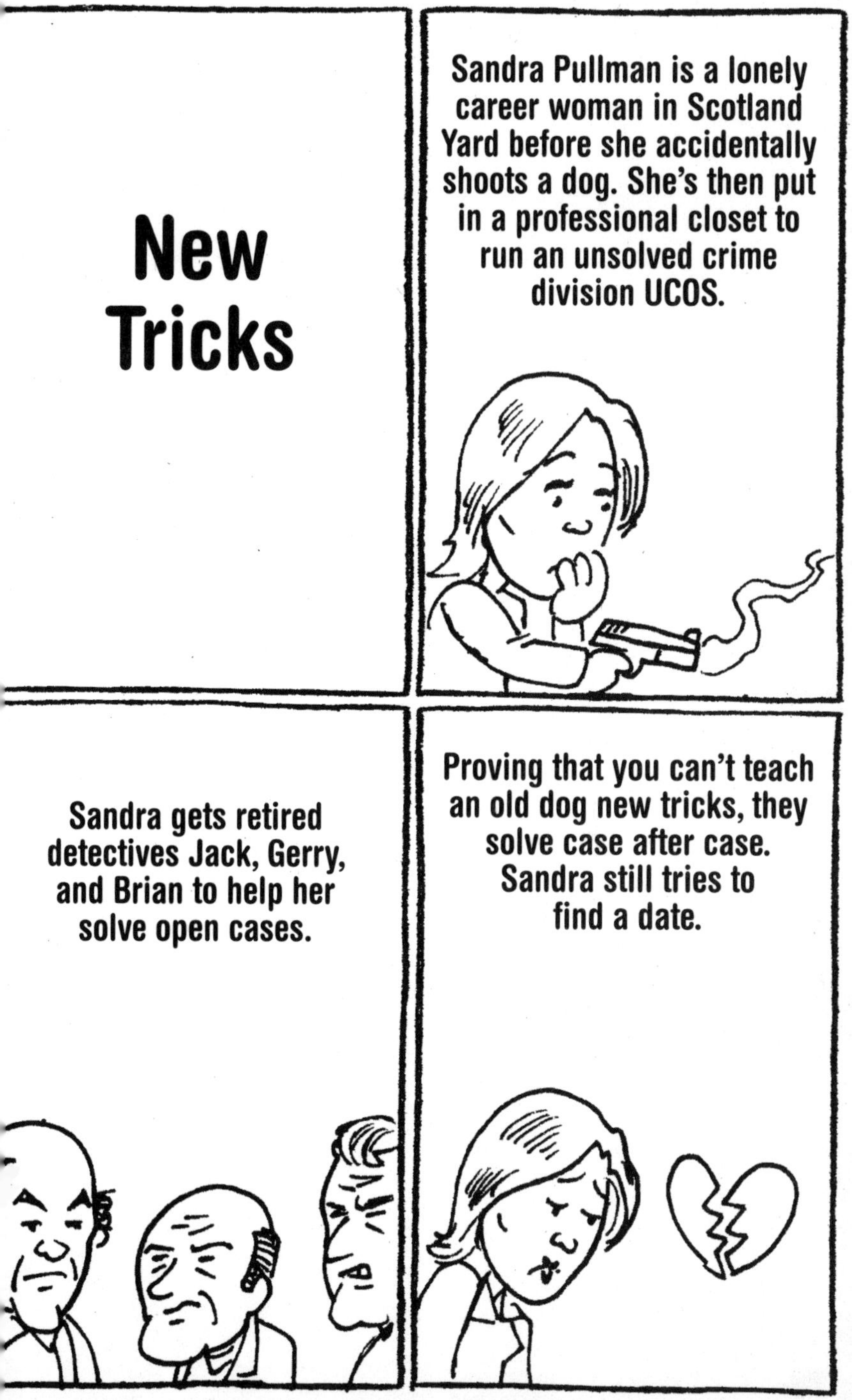
New Tricks
Sandra Pullman is a lonely career woman in Scotland Yard before she accidentally shoots a dog. She's then put in a professional closet to run an unsolved crime division UCOS.
Sandra gets retired detectives Jack, Gerry, and Brian to help her solve open cases.
Proving that you can't teach an old dog new tricks, they solve case after case. Sandra still tries to find a date.

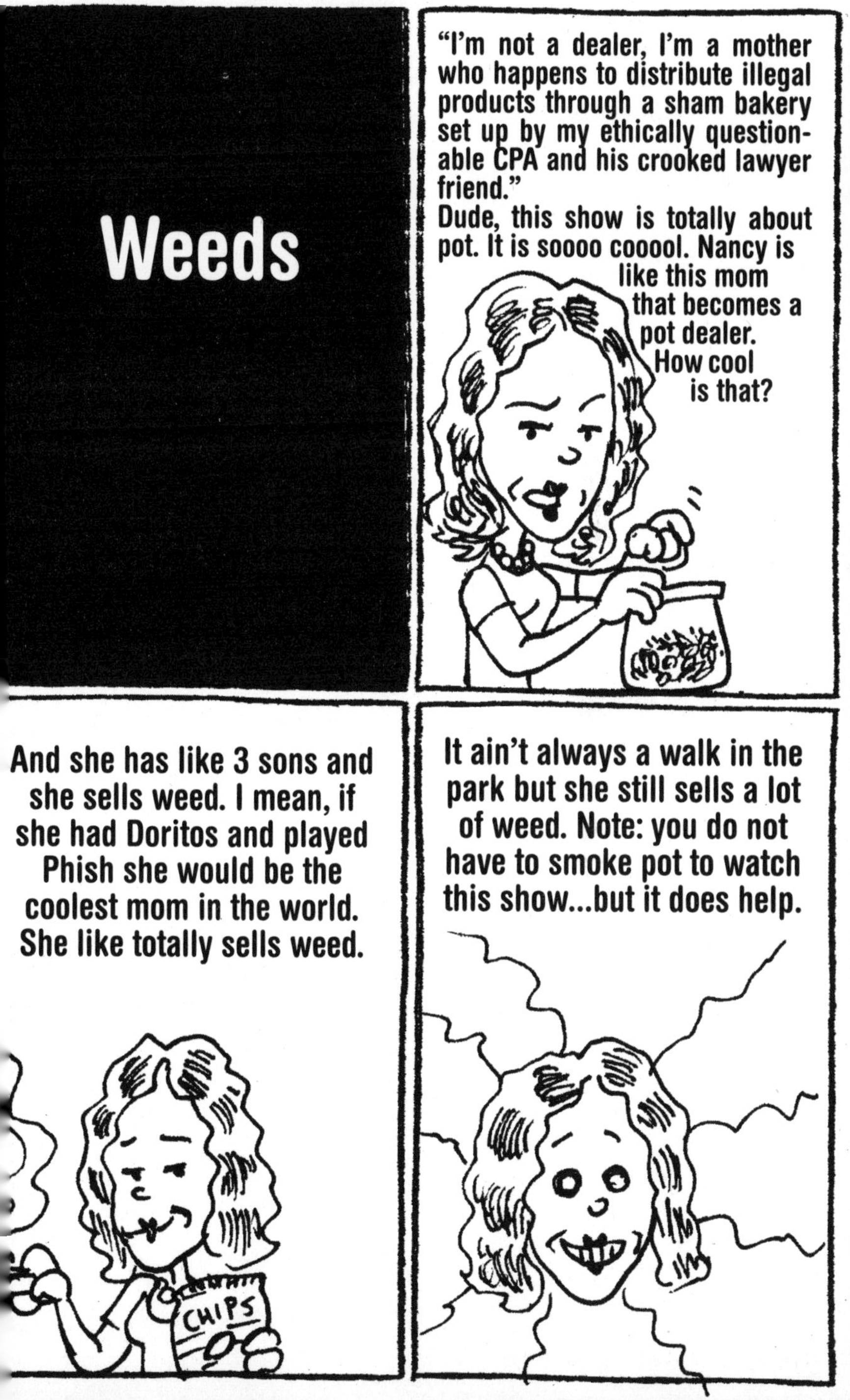
Weeds
"I'm not a dealer, I'm a mother who happens to distribute illegal products through a sham bakery set up by my ethically questionable CPA and his crooked lawyer friend."
Dude, this show is totally about pot. It is soooo cooool. Nancy is like this mom that becomes a pot dealer. How cool is that?
And she has like 3 sons and she sells weed. I mean, if she had Doritos and played Phish she would be the coolest mom in the world. She like totally sells weed.
CHIPS
It ain't always a walk in the park but she still sells a lot of weed. Note: you do not have to smoke pot to watch this show...but it does help.